Decline of the Public

Decline of the Public

The Hollowing-out of Citizenship

David Marquand

polity

First published in 2004 by Polity Press.

Reprinted 2004 (Twice), 2005

Polity Press
65 Bridge Street
Cambridge CB2 1UR, UK

Polity Press
350 Main Street
Malden, MA 02148, USA

ISBN: 0-7456 2909-1
ISBN: 0-7456 2910-5 (pb)

A catalogue record for this book is available from the British Library
and has been applied for from the Library of Congress.

Typeset in 11 on 13pt Sabon
by Graphicraft Limited, Hong Kong
Printed and bound in Great Britain by
Marston Book Services Limited, Oxford

For further information on Polity, visit our website: www.polity.co.uk

Contents

Acknowledgements

Even a short book can generate a long list of debts. I should therefore acknowledge my gratitude to my wife, Judith Marquand, who has been an unfailing source of ideas, advice and moral support; to Michael Freeden and Andrew Gamble for their helpful (indeed indispensable) comments on the original draft; and to Philip Aylett, Roger Bingham, Rodney Brazier, Liz Fisher, Will Hutton, Ben Page, Perri6 and the House of Commons Information Service for help on specific points. Last, but by no means least, I am immensely grateful to Ralf Dahrendorf, who first drew my attention to the concept of the public domain while I was serving, under his genial and stimulating chairmanship, on the Commission on Wealth Creation and Social Cohesion.

Prologue

Seen in historical perspective, the attempt to combine the equality of civil and political rights, which is of the essence of democracy, with the inequality of economic and social opportunities, which is of the essence of capitalism, is still in its first youth. There is sufficient experience, however, to suggest that the result represents, at best, a transitional arrangement. . . . The fatalism which foresees in Great Britain the inevitable clash of irreconcilable opponents, which has destroyed political civilisation in Germany and Italy, is clearly out of place. So also, however, is the light-hearted optimism which assumes that because so precarious an equipoise has maintained itself for half a century, it can be relied on with confidence to maintain itself for ever. It may well be the case that democracy and capitalism, which at moments in their youth were allies, cannot live together once both have come of age. (Tawney, Preface to 1938 edition of *Equality*)

This book is about the public domain – the domain of citizenship, equity and service whose integrity is essential to democratic governance and social well-being. I start from three interconnected propositions. The first is that the public domain has its own distinctive culture and decision rules. In it citizenship rights trump both market power and the bonds of clan or kinship. Professional pride in a job well done or a sense of civic duty or a mixture of both replaces the hope of

1

gain and the fear of loss (and, for that matter, loyalty to family, friends or dependants) as the spur to action. The second proposition is that the public domain is both priceless and precarious – a gift of history, which is always at risk. It can take shape only in a society in which the notion of a public interest, distinct from private interests, has taken root; and, historically speaking, such societies are rare breeds. Its values and practices do not come naturally, and have to be learned. Whereas the private domain of love, friendship and personal connection and the market domain of buying and selling are the products of nature, the public domain depends on careful and continuing nurture. The third proposition is that, in Britain, the last twenty years have seen an aggressively interventionist state systematically enfeebling the institutions and practices that nurtured it, and that it is now in crisis. The Hutton Inquiry took place after this book went to press, but it has shown how deep the crisis goes.

The single most important element of the New Right project of the 1980s and 1990s was a relentless *kulturkampf* designed to root out the culture of service and citizenship which had become part of the social fabric. De-regulation, privatization, so-called public–private partnerships, proxy markets, performance indicators mimicking those of the private corporate sector, and a systematic assault on professional autonomy narrowed the public domain and blurred the distinction between it and the market domain. Public functions of all kinds were farmed out to unaccountable appointed bodies, dominated by business interests and managed according to market principles. Intermediate institutions like the BBC, the universities, the schools, the museums and the health service were forced, so far as possible, into a market mould. So, above all, was the senior civil service, where the frontiers of the public domain had been most zealously guarded, and in which its values had been most thoroughly internalized. Meanwhile, the clamant rhetorics of private-sector management and public-choice economics corrupted

2

the language and undermined the self-confidence of the elites which had championed the public domain in happier days.

The dilapidated, over-stretched public services of twenty-first-century Britain are the most obvious legacy of this *kulturkampf*, but they are by no means the most dangerous one. Incessant marketization, pushed forward by the core executive at the head of the most centralized state in western Europe, has done even more damage to the public domain than low taxation and resource starvation. It has generated a culture of distrust, which is corroding the values of professionalism, citizenship, equity and service like acid in the water supply. For the marketizers, the professional, public-service ethic is a con. Professionals are self-interested rent-seekers, trying to force the price of their labour above its market value. The service ethic is a rhetorical device to legitimize a web of monopolistic cartels whose real purpose is to rip off the consumer. There is no point in appealing to the values of common citizenship. There are no citizens: there are only customers. Public servants cannot be trusted to give of their best. They are inherently untrustworthy. If they are allowed autonomy, they will abuse it. Like everyone else, they can be motivated only by sticks and carrots. If possible, privatization must expose them to the sticks and carrots of market competition. If not, they must be kept on their toes by repeated audits, assessments and appraisals.

Twenty years of this mean-spirited language and its accompanying measures have demoralized the public services and encouraged users who can afford it to buy their way out. The service ethic still has devoted champions among doctors, teachers, nurses, social workers, academics, broadcasters, judges, trade-union officials, local government staff and non-governmental organization workers. But danger signals are everywhere. The growing interpenetration of politics and business; the sleaze which has accompanied it; the dumbing down of the BBC and parts of the broadsheet press; the culture of private-sector sponsorship which has invaded public-domain institutions as varied as Oxbridge colleges, opera companies and in some places even the police; the diversion of academic energies from the pursuit of knowledge and the education of the young to a scrabble for advantage in mindless assessment exercises – all tell the same story. They show that the dykes our Victorian ancestors built to protect the public domain from invasion by the market domain have been breached at point after point. Even more damagingly, so does the virtual disappearance of the notion of a public interest, transcending private interests, from public debate.

The consequences go wider than appears at first sight. When Tawney wrote the passage I quoted at the start of this prologue, the threat to democracy came from overtly anti-democratic movements on the far right and left.[1] Though faint echoes of that threat can now be heard again in parts of continental Europe and in the United States and, for that matter, in certain English towns, the chief threat to democracy in present-day Britain is more insidious. It comes from what Colin Leys aptly calls 'market-driven politics',[2] from the steady retreat of the civic ideal in the face of the marketizers' *kulturkampf*. One of its manifestations is a secular decline in public confidence in political leaders, political parties and the whole political process. Another is a marked fall in electoral participation, particularly among the casualties of the capitalist renaissance of our day. The third and most serious is an ill-concealed, incomplete, but nevertheless unmistakable return to the politics of connection, favouritism and patronage which nineteenth-century Radicals labelled 'Old Corruption', and which the early champions of the public domain thought they had banished for ever. The forms of democracy survive, but its substance is becoming ever more attenuated. In the post-war heyday of the public domain, Tawney's fear that the 'equipoise' between market inequality and political equality might break down seemed far-fetched. After twenty years of incessant marketization, it seems, if anything, understated.

At this point a word of caution is in order. It is time to retrieve, or perhaps to reinvent the public domain. However, that does not imply a return to the public domain of old days. It had serious failings. Upright and conscientious though they were, the elites that ran its institutions were often aloof and condescending. Accountability was often lacking. Above all, the operational codes and tacit understandings of the central state were saturated with pre-democratic, essentially monarchical assumptions and values, which became increasingly out of joint with the attitudes of a better-educated and less deferential citizenry; and, as the state sank in esteem, the public domain all too often sank with it. These failings gave the marketizers their opportunity. They made headway in large part because they spoke to an unfocused, but widespread exasperation with the old elites and the old state, and to a popular demand for accountability. The public domain cannot be reinvented unless the causes of its recent tribulations are understood, and their lessons learned.

I have written this book in the hope that it will contribute to that process. In chapter 1, I begin by looking at three specific examples of the current malaise of the public domain. I then turn to a general discussion of the notion of the public domain. In chapter 2 I examine its lineage, and describe the long, complex process through which it developed in the second half of the nineteenth century and the first half of the twentieth. Chapter 3 strikes a more sombre note. It begins with a description of the public domain at its zenith, and then examines the forces which were already beginning to undermine it. In chapter 4 I try to account for the wave of marketization that transformed the political and moral economies in the final decades of the last century, and to describe, in broad outline, how it affected the institutions and practices of the public domain. In the final chapter I examine the record of the 'New' Labour governments of the present and recent past, sketch out the elements of a possible public philosophy for a reinvented public domain, and examine some of its implications.

1

Economical with the Actualité

On 12 October 1992 Paul Henderson, Trevor Abraham and Peter Allen, directors of the Midlands engineering firm Matrix Churchill, were brought to trial at the Old Bailey.[1] They were charged with dishonestly obtaining licences to export material intended for military use to Iraq by pretending that it would be used for civilian purposes. They claimed in their defence that the Government had been aware of the true purpose of the goods they wished to export (not least because Henderson, a long-standing MI6 informer, had revealed it to the intelligence services). They also claimed that at a meeting with the Machine Tools Technologies Association (MTTA) in January 1988 Alan Clark, then a Minister at the Department of Trade and Industry, had encouraged them to disguise it.

Before the trial opened, the defence lawyers sought discovery of a wide range of confidential Government records, including intelligence reports, minutes of meetings, and correspondence between officials and ministers, to substantiate their case. Despite the risk of a miscarriage of justice, strenuous attempts were made in Whitehall to keep the records confidential. Four ministers signed so-called public immunity certificates (PII certificates in the jargon) claiming that disclosure of most of the documents requested by the defence would be contrary to the public interest. The trial judge refused to accept the PII claims and ordered that the documents they covered should be disclosed to the defence. That was only the beginning of the prosecution's troubles. On 5 November, Alan Clark, by now out of Parliament, was cross-examined about his 1988 meeting with the MTTA. In one of the most extraordinary exchanges in recent British political history Clark admitted that he knew the Iraqi orders would be used to make munitions. Asked about the DTI note of the meeting, which recorded him as saying that the orders would be used for general engineering purposes, he answered,

> Well, it's our old friend being economical, isn't it?
> Q. With the truth?
> A. With the *actualité*. There was nothing misleading or dishonest to make a formal or introductory comment that the Iraqis would be using the current orders for general engineering purposes. All I didn't say was 'and for making munitions' . . .
> Q. You didn't want to let anyone know that at this stage these machines and their follow up orders were going to munitions factories to make munitions?
> A. No.
> Q. And the emphasis on peaceful purposes and general engineering and so on would help keep the matter confidential?
> A. I do not think it was principally a matter for public awareness. I think it was probably a matter for Whitehall cosmetics.[2]

Clark's evidence sank the prosecution case. The trial was adjourned until 9 November, when Alan Moses, the chief prosecution counsel, announced that the prosecution would be abandoned. The defendants were then acquitted.

Public Interest or Executive Convenience?

The collapse of the trial provoked a storm of indignation in Parliament and the press; to quell it, the beleaguered Prime Minister, John Major, appointed Sir Richard Scott, then a member of the Court of Appeal, to conduct an inquiry into the whole story of arms-related exports to Iraq. The inquiry took more than three years to complete; the eventual report ran to five volumes and more than 1,800 pages. Its immediate political impact was slight. Following a House of Commons debate in February 1996, the Government survived censure by one vote; the affair then passed into history. Yet its implications were profound. In minute detail, Scott traced the twists and turns of Government policy over a period of nearly ten years. He probed ministers' answers to Parliamentary Questions and their replies to MPs' letters. He subjected the run-up to the Matrix Churchill trial to exhaustive examination. He investigated related prosecutions, and examined the history of the legislation that gave the Government power to control exports in the first place. In doing all this, he threw a rare shaft of light on the inner workings of Whitehall – on the mentality of officialdom; on the relationship between civil servants and ministers; above all, on the executive's approach to Parliament and the public. He revealed a culture of secrecy and a structural temptation to duplicity that called the health of British democracy into question.

Two aspects of that culture stood out. The first had to do with the PII certificates. When the report was published, a good deal of legal argument took place about the state of PII law. In some quarters Scott was criticized for suggesting that the legal advice which had persuaded the ministers concerned to sign the certificates was unsound. But, for a non-lawyer, this is not the point. What matters is not the state of the law at the time the ministers signed; it is the mentality that led them and their officials to think that PII claims were appropriate at all. In drawing up and signing PII certificates, they were saying that it was more important for certain classes of official documents to be kept secret than for accused persons to have a fair trial. Only one of the ministers (Michael Heseltine) seemed concerned with the rights of the accused in criminal proceedings. The other ministers, and the officials who advised them, displayed a cavalier indifference to the possibility that, if the PII claims were upheld, innocent men might go to gaol. Behind that scandal lay a deeper one. Few would dispute that in certain policy areas, at any rate, the state may have secrets which it should be entitled to keep; that some official records may be so sensitive that they should not be disclosed, even if non-disclosure runs counter to fundamental legal principles. But the secrets involved in the Matrix Churchill case were not in this category. Disclosure posed no danger to the state. The public interest was not at stake – only the reputations of certain ministers and civil servants. The real purpose of the PII certificates was to protect the executive from embarrassment, not the public from harm. Whether in accordance with the then state of the law or not, the PII system was abused. The notion of the public interest was treated as a cover for executive convenience. In the process, the ethic of public service, whose vitality is essential to the public interest, was violated.

Even more disturbing than the story of the PII certificates were Scott's revelations about Whitehall's approach to Parliament. To appreciate their significance, the historical background needs to be sketched in. Government policy towards arms exports to Iraq was shaped by disparate pressures – the importance of the arms industry to the British economy, the shifting fortunes of the long Iran–Iraq War and the barbaric nature of the Iraqi regime. When the war broke out in 1980, Britain adopted a posture of neutrality, and the Government banned exports of 'lethal items' to both combatants. In December 1984 it adopted a more precise set of guidelines, emanating from the Foreign Secretary, Sir Geoffrey Howe. These reiterated the Government's refusal to supply lethal equipment to either side; stated that, subject to that 'overriding consideration', existing contracts would be honoured; added that orders for defence equipment which would 'significantly enhance the capability of either side to prolong or exacerbate the conflict' would not be approved in future; and concluded with a commitment to 'scrutinize rigorously' all applications for licences to export defence equipment to Iran and Iraq in line with this policy. These guidelines were not announced to Parliament, however, until October 1985, when they were made public in answer to a Parliamentary Question by Sir David Steel.

In August 1988, the Iran–Iraq War came to an end. The third guideline was now otiose: there was no longer a conflict to be prolonged or exacerbated. Meanwhile, prospects of lucrative contracts with the former combatants loomed. In Whitehall, pressure mounted to revise the Howe guidelines. Its chief source was the DTI, the sponsor department for the arms industry. In December 1988, after much prevarication and confusion, three middle-rank ministers – Clark, William Waldegrave of the Foreign Office, and Lord Trefgarne of the Ministry of Defence – agreed to a change in the third guideline. Instead of prohibiting the export of defence equipment which would 'significantly enhance the capability of either side to prolong or exacerbate the conflict', it now said that the prohibition should apply to exports 'which, in our view, would be of direct and significant assistance to either country in the conduct of offensive operations'. The change was more than semantic. The new policy was, and was intended to be, more liberal than the old. The ministers responsible for it also agreed, however, that it should not be announced to Parliament. Four months later, in April 1989, policy changed again, following Iran's proclamation of a *fatwah* against Salman Rushdie. Ministers now decided that the new, liberal regime should be applied only to Iraq; policy on arms exports to Iran would revert to the more stringent pre-1988 position. This latest change of policy, designedly discriminating in favour of Iraq, was also to be kept secret.

Secrecy was easier to proclaim than to preserve. Rumours of British arms sales to Iraq surfaced in the press. Concerned citizens wrote to their MPs. MPs wrote to ministers, and tabled questions in the House of Commons. To keep their post-cease-fire policies secret, ministers had to dissimulate. Scott devoted thirty-one pages of his report to Government statements on defence sales policy after the cease-fire.[3] With icy clarity, he showed that in 1989 and 1990 ministers wrote a total of more than seventy misleading letters to MPs, falsely implying (or in some cases stating) that Government policy on arms sales to Iran and Iraq had not been changed. He also showed that similarly misleading answers were given to a series of parliamentary questions. As he put it himself, these answers

> failed to inform Parliament of the current state of Government policy on non-lethal arms sales to Iraq. The failure was deliberate and was an inevitable result of the agreement between the three junior Ministers that no publicity would be given to the decision to adopt a more liberal, or relaxed, policy, or interpretation of the Guidelines, originally towards both Iran and Iraq and, later, towards Iraq alone. Having heard various explanations as to why it was necessary or desirable to withhold knowledge from Parliament and the public of the true nature of the Government's approach to the licensing of non-lethal defence sales to Iran and Iraq respectively, I have come to the conclusion that the overriding and determinative reason was a fear of strong public opposition to the loosening of restrictions on the supply of defence equipment to Iraq and a consequential fear that the pressure of the opposition might be detrimental to British trading interests.[4]

In short, ministers believed that their policies would not withstand parliamentary and public scrutiny. They therefore decided to disguise them. In the name of the public interest (and in the hope of promoting Britain's arms trade), they misled the public's elected representatives. In doing so, they flouted one of the fundamental axioms of parliamentary democracy – that the executive must be accountable to Parliament.

Mad Cows – Madder People?

The culture of secrecy was not confined to the arms trade. On 20 March 1996, three weeks after the Commons debate on the Scott Report, the Secretary of State for Health, Stephen Dorrell, told the House that ten young people had contracted a new variant of a fatal neurological disease, the Creutzfeldt–Jacob Disease (vCJD), and explained that they had probably been infected with Bovine Spongiform Encephalopathy (BSE), a fatal brain disease of cattle. In December 1997 the recently elected 'New' Labour Government appointed the Master of the Rolls, Lord Phillips, to head an inquiry into the whole affair.[5] When the Phillips Report was published in September 2000, there were eighty known cases of variant CJD in Britain. By May 2003 there had been ninety-six confirmed deaths from vCJD and thirty-three probable deaths. Given the length of the incubation period, there is no way of telling what the eventual toll will be. What is certain is that, for several years, Britain was the scene of a ruinous BSE epidemic, which endangered public health, inflicted enormous damage on her livestock industry and had no parallel elsewhere. Assuming that infected beef products are the source of vCJD, the chances are that more vCJD cases will appear in due course. Yet, for the best part of a decade, ministers and officials repeatedly insisted that there was no evidence that BSE could be transmitted to human beings, and that British beef was safe to eat. On one notorious occasion, the then Minister of Agriculture, John Gummer, was even filmed attempting to feed his four-year-old daughter, Cordelia, a hamburger. That was the most egregious episode in a prolonged official campaign to allay public anxieties that turned out to be well founded, but it was by no means the only one.

The story of the BSE crisis begins in December 1986, when the State Veterinary Service first identified the disease. It had never been seen before, and no one knew what caused it. It belonged to a class of diseases known as Transmissible Spongiform Encephalopathies (TSEs), which also included scrapie, a brain disease of sheep. It seemed reasonable to assume that cattle had contracted it from scrapie-infected meat and bone meal; since scrapie had been endemic in parts of Britain for centuries, and had caused no known damage to human health, this implied that the same would be true of BSE. In May 1988, the Ministry of Agriculture, Fisheries and Food (MAFF) banned the use of ruminant protein in ruminant feed (the ruminant feed ban). Meanwhile, it set up a working party, chaired by Sir Richard Southwood, to examine all the ramifications of the BSE outbreak, including its implications for human health. At its first meeting, the working party recommended that the carcasses of infected animals should be destroyed, so as to ensure that they did not enter the human food chain; this was accepted. In February 1989 it produced its report. It accepted the scrapie theory, and judged that the risk that BSE could be transmitted to humans was 'remote'. It added, however, that if its assessment of the risk turned out to be wrong, 'the implications would be extremely serious'. It also recommended that certain bovine offals should be excluded from baby food – thus implying that 'remote' did not mean 'non-existent'. In November 1989 MAFF brought in a Specified Bovine Offals (SBO) ban prohibiting the use of these offals, not just in baby food, but in all human food.

The scrupulous qualifications of the Southwood Committee's Report were soon lost from sight. MAFF opinion hardened into a dogma. The Government's scientists had said there was no evidence that BSE could be transmitted to human beings. Ergo, beef must be safe to eat. Scientists who took a different view were not consulted. Outside critics were contemptuously dismissed. Unfortunately, the epidemic turned out to be far more serious than anyone had foreseen. When the working party reported in February 1989, BSE cases were running at 400 a month. By the end of the year, more than 10,091 cases had been confirmed. By the end of 1990, the figure had risen to 24,396. In September 1990, MAFF extended the SBO ban from human to animal food. But this was the age of de-regulation, when, as the Phillips Report put it coyly, '[e]nforcement was expected to be done with a light touch'.[6] That was an understatement. De-regulation had become a shibboleth in Whitehall; and it soon became clear that MAFF's regulatory regime left ample scope for evasion. By 1991 BSE had spread to cattle born after the ruminant feed ban – showing that the ban had been evaded or was ineffective. There was growing evidence of non-compliance with the SBO ban as well; in 1995 a spot check revealed that more than half the slaughterhouses visited were failing to observe the regulations then in force. Meanwhile, new evidence called Southwood's estimate of the risk to human life into question. In laboratory conditions, BSE was transmitted to mice, and later to a pig. In March 1990, a domestic cat developed BSE-like symptoms, suggesting that BSE could cross the species barrier more easily than scrapie, and not only in a laboratory. By September 1994, fifty-six other cats had followed suit. In 1993, two dairy farmers died of vCJD. A third died of it in 1994, and a fourth developed it in 1995. Cases of BSE had appeared in all their herds.

Privately, one or two Government scientists began to have second thoughts about the transmissibility of BSE to human beings. However, these did not penetrate the MAFF bunker. Officialdom clung to the dogma of the early days. In the months leading up to Dorrell's statement explaining that the new vCJD cases had probably been caused by BSE-infected beef, the Cabinet decided to respond to growing public anxieties with the familiar refrain that its professional advisers had assured it that the disease could be transmitted to humans'. The Meat and Livestock Commission (MLC), a quango whose task was to promote efficiency in the livestock industry, ran a hard-hitting advertising campaign designed to bolster beef sales. Dorrell himself said on television that there was 'no conceivable risk' from eating beef. The Chief Medical Officer insisted that there was 'no scientific evidence of a link between meat eating and development of CJD', and that 'beef was safe to eat', adding for good measure that he would continue to eat it himself. The Chief Medical Officer for Scotland declared that the Government's 'scientific advisers are saying consistently that there is no evidence at all that eating beef or other foods derived from beef is dangerous'.[7]

These assurances were part of a syndrome going back to the beginning of the epidemic. As the Phillips Report put it, throughout ministers and officials 'followed an approach whose object was sedation', shaped by 'a consuming fear of provoking an irrational public scare'.[8] This was not because they deliberately set out to deceive. It was because,

> [a]lthough most of those concerned with handling BSE ... understood the available science as indicating that the likelihood that BSE posed a risk [to humans] was remote, they did not trust the public to adopt as sanguine an attitude. Ministers, officials and scientific advisory committees alike were all apprehensive that the public would react irrationally to BSE. As each additional piece of data about the disease became available, the fear was that it would cause disproportionate alarm, would be seized on by the media and by dissident scientists as demonstrating that BSE was a danger to humans, and would lead to a food scare or, even more serious, a vaccine scare.[9]

In short, 'we', ministers, civil servants and Government-approved scientists, were by definition rational. 'They', the public, were not. And if 'they' disagreed with 'us', that only proved how irrational 'they' were. Or, as Stephen Dorrell put it in a television programme, it was the people, not the cows, who were mad.[10]

The consequences were both perverse and tragic. The sedation may or may not have calmed the general public, but it almost certainly had a significant effect on inspectors, slaughterhouse managements, and MAFF officials themselves. The Government's campaign of reassurance was based on the assumption that the measures it had taken to minimize BSE risks would be fully implemented and vigorously enforced. But that crucial premise went almost unmentioned in ministerial and advisory committee statements. Ministers did not say that the risks *would be* remote *if* their precautionary measures were observed; they only said that the risks were remote. As a result, the campaign blunted the zeal of those who had to implement and enforce the measures on which it was predicated. Why go out of one's way to enforce every last jot and tittle of a tiresome and unpopular regulation if the risks it was supposed to guard against did not exist?

There was a deeper perversity as well. Ministers were caught in a vicious circle of their own making. They distrusted the public; and they believed that the public distrusted them. That was one of the reasons why they were so anxious to shelter behind their scientific advisers. But because they distrusted the public, their campaign of sedation ended by exacerbating the distrust which it was designed to counter. In discussion with the Phillips committee, the Government's chief scientific adviser, Sir Robert May, argued that instead of taking 'a simple message out into the market place . . . the full messy process whereby scientific understanding is arrived at with all its problems has to be spilled out into the open'.[11] Because it was terrified of public irrationality, the Government did very nearly the opposite. Science was treated as an oracle, even as a bludgeon, not as a process. When the oracle turned out to be wrong, and the bludgeon lost its power, public confidence was still further undermined.

The BSE epidemic and the vCJD outbreak it brought in its train were not scandalous in the sense that the Arms to Iraq affair was scandalous. Ministers and officials did not mislead Parliament or the public about the true nature of their policies. Their downfall came partly because they insisted on treating the inherently provisional judgements of their scientific advisers as fixed and permanent truths, and then over-simplified them grossly for public consumption, and partly because the fetish for de-regulation pulled against the public interest in safe food. Consumers and farmers paid dearly for officialdom's hubristic scientism and ideological fixations, but the latter cannot be equated with the furtive evasions anatomized in the Scott Report. Yet both episodes had important features in common. The DTI's role as sponsor for arms exporters was paralleled by MAFF's as sponsor for farmers, so that in both cases powerful private economic interests bore heavily on the guardians of the public interest.[12] (To take a particularly gross example, in the early stages of the epidemic, scientists in the State Veterinary Service were forbidden to publish articles about BSE, in the belief that publicity might damage British exports.) On a deeper level, both reflected the inward-looking culture of the British state, which instinctively operates on the 'need to know' principle. (Those who need to know, know; those who don't know, don't need to know, and therefore should not be told.) On a deeper level still, both had to do with trust and the break-down of trust – with government's unwillingness to trust the public, and the erosion of public trust in government – and thereby with the fundamentals of democratic citizenship. At the heart of the BSE crisis lay one of the most intractable problems of modern governance: the problem of how to assess and manage risk in accordance with democratic norms. The ministers and officials concerned made a mess of it. Not the least of the reasons why is that they too were enmeshed in the culture of secrecy which had played such a malign part in the Arms to Iraq affair.

Stitch-up

The culture of secrecy was (and is) blood brother to a culture of central control, whose manifestations were (and are) omnipresent. One of the most piquant recent examples concerned that Cinderella of British democracy, local government. In May 1997, a few months before Lord Phillips began the BSE inquiry, Tony Blair's 'new' Labour Party entered office committed to a 'democratic renewal'. Scotland was to have a Parliament, with extensive legislative powers; Wales was to have a less powerful elected Assembly. In general, Labour's approach to local government was much more cautious, but there was one striking exception. In 1986 the Thatcher Government had abolished the Greater London Council, following a succession of bruising battles with its left-Labour leader, the flamboyant, charismatic and infuriatingly cheeky 'Red Ken' Livingstone. Since then, there had been no London-wide local authority, only thirty-two separate London boroughs, and a web of quangos. Thanks largely to Blair's personal enthusiasm, Labour's 1997 election manifesto promised a complete break with the past. If the London electorate approved the proposal in a referendum, the capital would be governed by a directly elected executive mayor, scrutinized by an elected assembly. On 7 May 1998 the referendum duly took place. In a low poll, Londoners voted for a directly elected mayor by a margin of 72 per cent to 28 per cent. Legislation establishing an elected mayor and assembly (the Greater London Assembly, or GLA) was passed in 1999.

By then, attention had shifted from the constitution of the new London authority to a bitter, yet at times farcical, struggle for the mayoralty. Blair and his advisers seem to have hoped that London's new governance system would give birth to a new kind of municipal politician – dynamic, entrepreneurial, charismatic and more reminiscent of Richard Branson than of the solid party wheel-horses who normally congregated in the nation's town halls.[13] The outcome could hardly have been more ironic. At first, the Conservative candidate was Jeffrey Archer – not exactly a second Branson, but undeniably dynamic. Unfortunately, he had to abandon his candidature when it emerged that he had persuaded a friend to give him a false alibi in connection with the *Daily Star*'s allegation that he had slept with a prostitute. He was succeeded by Steve Norris, another colourful figure, but a truthful one. However, the embarrassments which the Conservatives suffered in their search for a candidate were as nothing compared to the Labour Party's. No Branson-like figure came forward. Instead, the front runner for the Labour nomination was Thatcher's tormentor, 'Red Ken' Livingstone, now a Labour backbench MP. As it happened, Livingstone had many of the qualities that Blair hoped to see in Britain's first directly elected mayor. He was undeniably charismatic, and patently dynamic. Arguably, he was also entrepreneurial. But, from Downing Street's point of view, he had the wrong kind of charisma. He had mellowed in the eleven years since the abolition of the GLC, but he was as irreverent as ever, and his carefully polished one-liners were as deadly. Worse yet, he still called himself a socialist, and appeared to mean it. Unlike other 1980s leftists who had seen the error of their ways and received preferment for doing so, he gave no sign of repenting of his past. To Blair and his colleagues, he symbolized all that was wrong with the so-called loony left councils of the 1980s. He was wild, irresponsible, disloyal and (worst of all) an electoral albatross. A Livingstone candidacy would put at risk all that Blair had done to banish the memory of the bad old days of sectarianism, schism and unelectability. At all costs, Livingstone had to be denied the Labour nomination.

The costs were high. Possible alternatives to Livingstone were few and unimpressive. Unsuccessful approaches were made to the independent MP Martin Bell. There were rumours that the lightning would strike Pauline Green, leader of the Socialist Group in the European Parliament. There was talk of Mo Mowlam. The well-known black broadcaster, Trevor Phillips, put his hat into the ring, as did Glenda Jackson, the former actress and present MP for Hampstead. At a late stage in the proceedings, they were followed by Nick Raynsford, a London MP and impeccably Blairite junior minister. But Raynsford's hopes were dashed when, after much hesitation and prevarication, Frank Dobson resigned his Cabinet post as Health Secretary and announced his candidature. Raynsford and Phillips then withdrew, and threw such weight as they had behind Dobson.

The party leadership now had its candidate for the nomination. The trouble was that party members seemed unlikely to vote for him. Meanwhile, the Livingstone threat loomed ever larger. The leadership reacted in two ways. It set up a panel of party loyalists, chaired by Clive Soley, the chairman of the parliamentary Labour Party, to vet all the candidates for the nomination. Livingstone was asked repeatedly if he would promise to fight on the party's still-unwritten manifesto, but in an adroitly worded statement he refused to give the leadership a blank cheque. He was, he said, 'perfectly aware that Labour candidates stand on the manifesto democratically agreed by the party'. But he added ominously,

> The Labour Party stands for the devolution of power to the people and democratic control of local government. The Labour Party in Scotland has entered a coalition with the Liberal Democrats. In Wales, Labour has formed a minority administration. Those decisions were taken in Scotland and Wales, not Westminster. Devolution means that how we regenerate London's transport system is a decision for Londoners.[14]

Despite Livingstone's refusal to eat humble pie, the panel reluctantly decided to allow his candidature for the nomination to go forward, fearing mass resignations from the party if it refused to do so.

The panel interrogations were only a skirmish; the real battle was still to come. The ground on which it was fought had been assiduously tended by Livingstone's enemies. Until Dobson threw his hat into the ring in October 1999, the universal assumption was that Labour would choose its mayoral candidate by OMOV – one member, one vote. But by then it was clear that, in an OMOV selection, Livingstone would win. In normal circumstances, Blair and his associates would almost certainly have favoured OMOV. It was modern, democratic and transparent. As such, it marked a break from the murky election processes associated with Old Labour. But, in comparison with the leadership's adamantine determination to stop Livingstone, these attractions counted for nothing. No sooner had Dobson announced his decision to stand than the party's National Executive decided that Labour's candidate for the mayoralty would be selected by an electoral college composed of three sections with equal voting strength – Labour MPs, MEPs and GLA candidates; trade unions and other affiliated organizations; and individual party members. For good measure, it also decided that the unions would not be obliged to ballot their own members before casting their votes. It was a classic Old Labour stitch-up, of exactly the sort Labour modernizers were supposed to be against. In the short term, it served its purpose. Livingstone was far ahead in the individual member section, and slightly ahead in the trade-union section, but Dobson's overwhelming lead in the section for MPs, MEPs and GLA candidates put him fractionally ahead in the electoral college as a whole. In the longer term, Dobson's victory availed him nothing. Livingstone could justifiably complain that the party machine had stolen the selection; after some hesitation he announced that he would stand for the mayoralty as an independent (breaking an oft-repeated promise not to do so). On 5 May 2000 he was triumphantly elected, albeit only after the second preferences of the bottom nine candidates had been taken into account. The Conservative, Steve Norris, was a good second. Dobson came a bad third in the first count, and was therefore excluded from the second count. Nothing quite like it had been seen since Dick Taverne's crushing victory as an independent in the Lincoln by-election in 1973.

Livingstone had beaten the Labour Party machine, but he had not beaten the Labour Government. The central issue in the mayoral election was the state of the London Under-ground and the way to finance long-overdue investment in its crumbling infrastructure. In the 1997 general election the

Conservatives fought on the ticket of Tube privatization. The Labour manifesto rejected 'wholesale privatization' and committed the party to 'a new public/private partnership to improve the Underground, safeguard the public interest and guarantee value for money to taxpayers'.[15] However, the form of this mysterious new partnership was not specified; and it was not until Labour entered office that ministers decided what meaning to give the term. As so often, they followed where their predecessors had led. The Major Government had launched a 'private finance initiative' (PFI) designed to tap private capital for public infrastructure projects. The principles were straightforward. Private companies would make the necessary investment and bear part of the risk involved. Payment would be spread over several years. At the end of that period, the assets would revert to full public ownership. In the interim they would be available for use by the relevant part of the public sector. It was rather like a hire-purchase agreement: use now, pay later. For ministers anxious to keep taxes low, the beauty of PFI was that, under Treasury rules, the investments did not count towards the public sector borrowing requirement. Another alleged advantage was that the private companies concerned were bound to be more efficient than the public sector, so that the taxpayer would get better value for money. These considerations weighed as heavily with the new Government as with the old. Fatally, the public–private partnership (PPP) it devised for the London Underground was modelled on the Conservatives' PFI.

'Son of PFI'[16] was a much more complex animal than its parent. The trains would still be run by London Underground, which would soon become a subsidiary of a new body called Transport for London (TfL). The track would be handed over in three sections to private infrastructure companies ('infracos'), which would maintain and improve it. The infracos would also be responsible for maintaining and renewing the trains at night, when they would not be in service. At the end of a period – at first of fifteen years, but later extended to thirty – ownership of the track would revert to

TfL. The payments to the infracos would be determined by their success in achieving specified outputs. The benchmarks for calculating success would be based on extraordinarily arcane and necessarily contestable assumptions about the Tube's performance under public ownership. This delicate structure contained two gaping holes. If the contracts with the infracos were too generous, as a wide range of outside experts believed them to be, risk would not be transferred from the public to the private sector after all, and the taxpayer would not get better value for money. Worse still, experience of the privatized railway system showed that separating the track from the trains could have disastrous consequences for safety. (The notorious Ladbroke Grove train crash, which killed thirty-one people and injured 425, took place in October 1999, when the hapless Dobson began his campaign for the Labour nomination for the mayoralty. The Hatfield crash, which rubbed home the dangers of splitting responsibility, occurred a year later.)

Opposition to the PPP was the central plank of Livingstone's election campaign. Susan Kramer, the Liberal Democrat candidate, was also opposed. Steve Norris was for outright privatization of the Tube. Once elected, Livingstone insisted – with justice – that the PPP had been rejected by a massive majority of London's voters. This cut no ice with the Government. Nor did a sceptical report by the House of Commons Select Committee on Transport. Livingstone himself commissioned the Industrial Society, directed by Will Hutton, to review the issues. The Hutton Report, published in September 2000, concluded that the PPP should go ahead 'only if it meets much more rigorous safety and value-for-money criteria, and if it is substantially amended to protect against the risk that the contracts are incomplete and overgenerous'.[17] Once again, the Government was unmoved. With characteristic chutzpah, Livingstone appointed Robert Kiley, a tough former CIA officer who had turned around the New York subway system, as Transport Commissioner for London. Kiley condemned the PPP contracts; argued that the necessary investment could be financed partly by operating surpluses and partly by borrowing against future income; and insisted that managerial control over the entire system should remain with London Underground. Despite rumours of a compromise, the Government refused to budge. Livingstone twice tried to stop the PPP through judicial review, but the courts were powerless to intervene. In a last, desperate throw he took the issue to the European Court, but there too the Government won. Meanwhile, the contracts with the infracos, which had been over-generous in the first place, became even more favourable to them. In the end, the PPP turned out to be more expensive than the public sector alternative would have been. On the Government's own criteria, it should have been rejected.

In this tangled story, three themes stand out. The first has to do with democracy and decentralization. The Government said it wished to 'renew' British democracy. Blair proclaimed the virtues of 'open, vibrant, diverse democratic debate' on the local level. But when the debate took a turn that ministers and officials disliked, they made frantic efforts to stifle it. They took it for granted that their PPP offered the best solution to the problems of the London Underground, and that was that. The views of London's mayor and voters were immaterial. As in the Arms to Iraq affair and the BSE crisis, ministers knew best. Because they knew best, they made a nonsense of their own decentralization project. The second and third themes go deeper. There was a curiously frenzied quality about ministers' commitment to PPP. No doubt, part of the reason for their refusal to budge was that they were determined to punish Livingstone for crushing their mayoral candidate at the polls. Yet it is hard to believe that this is the whole explanation. They were motivated by ideological principle as well as personal pique. PPP was (or at least appeared to be) a market solution, and New Labour was committed to market solutions with all the zeal of a convert. Last, but by no means least, the Treasury was, and in modern times always has been, an instinctively centralist institution, viscerally suspicious of lower tiers of government and hostile to suggestions that they should be given more autonomy. A victory for Livingstone would have been a defeat for the Treasury, and for the Chancellor of the Exchequer as its head. As such, it would have sent a dangerous message to other uppity local politicians. If only *pour encourager les autres*, he had to be humiliated. In comparison, local democracy, public safety and even value for money hardly counted.

Themes

The story I have told so far is more like a picaresque tale than a carefully plotted novel. It boasts a huge cast list, and covers a wide range of topics. Yet certain common themes weave in and out of it, albeit in different guises. In one way or another, each of my three episodes has to do with the public interest, public trust, public goods, and the public sphere of collective action and democratic accountability. Each also raises disturbing questions about the relationship between that sphere and the sphere of competitive market competition, on the one hand, and the state, on the other. In the first episode we saw ministers and civil servants taking it for granted that they had the exclusive right to define the public interest, and a corresponding right to mislead the public and its elected representatives about the policies they had derived from their definition. We also saw that they diminished democratic accountability – one of the supreme public goods – in the process. In the second, ministers, officials and their chosen scientific advisers botched an admittedly tricky case of the politics of risk because they did not trust the public to react rationally to a full account of the risks in question – in other words, because they took it for granted that they were better qualified than the public to decide what risks the public should run. For their pains, they further undermined public trust in government. In the third, the incoming Labour Government embarked on a novel, if half-hearted experiment in municipal democracy and local autonomy for the capital, only to discover to its horror that voters and party members alike supported a charismatic critic of the party leadership, and favoured a solution to the long-standing problems of the London Underground which ran counter to that of the central state. Though the leadership rigged the selection process, its candidate was crushingly defeated in the subsequent election. Ministers reacted by forcing their own complex and costly quasi-privatization scheme down the throats of the successful candidate and the voters who had elected him.

The implications go wide, and I shall explore some of them more fully in later chapters. For the moment, I mention only two. The story I have just tried to summarize is quintessentially a story of the *public domain* – of the domain where the public interest is defined and public goods produced. In varying ways, the episodes I have described all help to show that it is now in jeopardy.

Definitions

At this point, some definitions are in order. The public domain, in my sense of the term, should not be confused with the public sector. It depends on public institutions (notably the rule of law), but it is not confined to them. In principle, a large public domain could coexist with a small public sector. There is certainly nothing sacrosanct about the ratio between the two which obtained in mid- and late-twentieth-century Britain. In earlier periods, the ratio was very different; and there is no reason of principle why it should not be different in future. As I shall show in the next chapter, the growth of the public domain provides one of the central themes of nineteenth-century British history. For most of that period, the public sector grew much more slowly. Government expenditure as a proportion of GNP was lower in 1900 than it had been in 1831, and in absolute terms it did not grow very much until the decade of the 1890s.[18] As late as the 1920s, Keynes expected further growth in the public domain (not that he used the term) – not as a result of state action, but because privately owned companies would increasingly assume public responsibilities. The Bank of England (then still in private ownership) was already a classic case of such a company. In the 1950s, Anthony Crosland, the high priest of the revisionist social democracy of the day, thought one of the reasons why capitalism had changed so radically that it could hardly be called capitalism any longer was that the managers of big capitalist firms increasingly adopted a public-service ethic.

Indeed, the public domain should not be seen as a 'sector' at all. It is best understood as a dimension of social life, with its own norms and decision rules, cutting across sectoral boundaries: as a set of activities, which can be (and historically have been) carried out by private individuals, private charities and even private firms as well as public agencies. It is symbiotically linked to the notion of a public interest, in principle distinct from private interests; central to it are the values of citizenship, equity and service. In it goods are distributed on the basis of need and not of personal ties or access to economic resources. It is a space, protected from the adjacent market and private domains, where strangers encounter each other as equal partners in the common life of the society – a space for forms of human flourishing which cannot be bought in the market-place or found in the tight-knit community of the clan or family or group of intimates. In a memorable account of the growth of social citizenship in the post-war period, T. H. Marshall wrote that its real significance lay, not in promoting income equality, but in 'a general enrichment of the concrete substance of civilised life . . . an equalisation between the more and the less fortunate at all levels'.[19] He was writing about the post-war welfare state, but he caught the essence of the public domain as such.

In it, citizenship rights trump both market power and kinship or neighbourhood bonds; the duties of citizenship take precedence both over market incentives and over private loyalties. As the Dahrendorf Commission put it,

> The private world of love and friendship, and the market world of interest and incentive, are not the only dimensions of human life in society. There is a public domain with its own values. . . . In the public domain people act neither out of the kindness of their hearts, nor in response to incentives, monetary or otherwise, but because they have a sense of serving the community.[20]

That, of course, is an ideal, and a demanding ideal at that. No one could pretend that it is always followed in practice. Indeed, part of the point of the story I told earlier in this chapter is to show how, in recent years, it has been badly flouted by civil servants and by politicians of both major parties. But this does not mean that the ideal is in some way unreal or irrelevant: the same applies to the norms of the market domain and the private domain. Sellers sometimes collude to do down buyers, and friends are sometimes false, but it does not follow that the market and private domains are in some sense normless. The important point is that the ideal is distinct and, so to speak, autonomous: that the norms governing behaviour in the public domain and the practices that embody and sustain them; the quality and character of the human relationships engendered in it; the principles that govern access to the activities that are carried on in it; and the incentives and disincentives that affect those who carry them on *differ* from their equivalents in the market and private domains.

In the private domain, loyalty to friends and family is a (perhaps *the*) supreme virtue. In the public domain, it is not. E. M. Forster's famous assertion that he would rather betray his country than his friends was shocking because he had applied the norms of the private domain to a domain where they do not belong. Favouritism and nepotism are shocking for the same reason. To apply the values of the private domain to the public domain is, in a profound sense, to corrupt it. It is equally shocking, because equally corrupting, to apply market norms to the public domain. That is why it is a crime to buy and sell votes or honours or government policies or justice. In the market domain, goods and services are – quite properly – commodities to be bought and sold. The price mechanism allocates resources, including labour. In principle at least, free competition ensures that they are allocated efficiently. But votes, honours, government policies and justice belong to the public domain. And because they belong to the public domain, they must not be commodified. By the same token, the measuring rods that assess efficiency in the market domain – 'throughput', productivity, added value, the monetary return on capital – have no place in the public domain. Academics do not miraculously become more efficient when the staff–student ratio falls and lectures are overcrowded; the value of a stay in hospital is not enhanced if low-paid contract nurses, with little commitment to the job, replace established nursing teams.

Boundaries

Much of this is obviously very fuzzy. Part of the point of this book is to open up a debate which will, I hope, yield greater precision in future; but for the moment boundary problems proliferate. One tricky problem concerns the frontier between the public and the market domains. Certain occupations – policemen, civil servants, judges, soldiers – normally belong to the public domain. Others – foreign exchange dealers, supermarket managers, software designers, pop musicians – inhabit the market domain. But many cross the frontier between the two. In one optic, barristers are market traders, selling their wares in a highly competitive market-place, where rents of ability can be very high. But that is not all they are. They also have duties to the Court. Their primary duty is to ensure that justice is fairly and impartially administered; and that duty is supposed to override their economic interests. Trade unions also sell their wares – or rather their members' wares – in the market-place. They exist to screw the highest possible price for their members' labour power out of potential purchasers. But in doing this they mitigate what Keynes famously called 'the theory of the economic juggernaut'[21] in the name of the non-market principle of the just price; in doing so they also promote the public good of industrial citizenship. In the days before the 1911 National Insurance Act, most doctors earned their living from privately paid fees. But many doctors adjusted their fee schedules to their patients' ability to pay, and they did so because they subscribed, at least to some degree and in some cases, to a public-service ethic. Before universities were funded by the state, academic salaries were paid from the university's fee income. Despite charitable benefactions which financed scholarships for the exceptionally talented, access to a university education was largely confined to those who could pay for it. But academics also adhered (or tried intermittently to adhere) to a public-service ethic which told them to promote the public goods of disinterested learning, a qualified elite and the transmission of high culture to the young. These values decreed a meritocratic examination system, and ruled out the sale of degrees.

To decide who and what belong to the public domain, then, we have to look at providers as well as at what they provide. Most of all, we have to look at the ethic or ethics that motivate providers, and at the institutions and practices which embody and transmit those ethics. Doctors, lawyers, educators, trade-union bargainers are not rationally calculating market actors, behaving in accordance with the profit motive – or, at any rate, not solely. At least in principle, they are supposed to abide by an ethic of public service that tells them to pursue the public interest, even if they earn their livings in a market of some sort. They are not agents of their clients alone. They are also the agents of the public at large. Of course, they may fail to discharge their public-service obligations, but if they do, they dishonour their vocation.

Another problem, which provides one of the central themes of this book, has to do with the relationship between the public domain and the state. At first sight, the two can easily be confused: after all, the public domain is the domain of citizenship, and states have citizens. A closer look yields a much more complex picture. For most of the last 120 years, most activities of the British state have been part of the public domain. The officials who have carried them out have also belonged to it. This has not always been true, however. In Europe, at any rate, the state came before the public domain. Henry VIII, Elizabeth I, Philip II, Francis I, and the other leading monarchs of early-modern Europe ruled powerful and imposing states, but they did not acknowledge a public interest transcending private interests. Still less did they acknowledge any obligation to pursue it. The 'kingly state', as Philip Bobbitt calls it,[22] was an emanation of the sovereign (*L'état c'est moi*, Louis XIV famously declared), not a separate entity standing above both ruler and ruled. More than 300 years later, the totalitarian party-states of the twentieth century were emanations of the party and the leader. They perverted the service ethic of the public domain into an instrument of party control, colonized its institutions and remodelled its practices to fit party imperatives. Both in Hitler's Germany and in Stalin's Soviet Union, in other words, the state effectively destroyed the public domain – not that Tsarist Russia had had much of a public domain before the revolution. As I try to show in the next two chapters, the record of the British state is ambiguous. In the second half of the nineteenth century and the first half of the twentieth, it was, on the whole, a friend of the public domain, though on occasion an overbearing one. But it became a friend only because the early champions of the public domain radically reconstructed it; and in the final decades of the twentieth century a second reconstruction turned it into an enemy. Even in its friendly phase, moreover, the centralist, power retentive instincts it was to manifest during the BSE crisis and the battles over the London Underground made it a less whole-hearted friend than champions of the public domain always recognized. For the public domain is quintessentially the realm of engagement, debate and contestation. The pre-democratic, monarchical traditions of the British state have always been in tension with the need for social spaces in which these can flourish.

A Gift of History

In spite of fuzziness and boundary problems, two points stand out. The first is that the public domain is fundamental to a civilized society. (It is not an accident that 'civilize' and 'citizen' come from the same root.) This does not mean that it is fundamental to society as such. Most societies, through most of human history, have lacked a public domain; in most societies, there has been no public to *have* a domain. There have been rulers and ruled, monarchs and subjects, lords and serfs, masters and servants, owners and slaves, priests and lay people, classes and masses. And, of course, there have always been buyers and sellers. But these did not – could not – make a public. There were no citizens, and therefore no space where citizens could engage with each other. Because there was no space for citizenship, or the rights and duties of citizenship, the notion of a public interest could have no meaning. The private domain has always been with us; and Adam Smith was probably right in thinking that the 'truck, barter and exchange' of the market domain are natural to human beings. But there is nothing natural about the public domain. It is a gift of history, and of fairly recent history at that.

It is literally a priceless gift. The goods of the public domain cannot be valued by market criteria, but they are no less precious for that. They include fair trials, welcoming public spaces, free public libraries, subsidized opera, mutual building societies, safe food, the broadcasts of the BBC World Service, the lobbying of Amnesty International, clean water, impartial public administration, disinterested scholarship,

32

blood donors, magistrates, the minimum wage, the Pennine Way and the rulings of the Health and Safety Executive. Less obviously, they also include liberty – not in the familiar sense of freedom to pursue private interests, but in the classical republican sense of freedom from domination. In the public domain, market power is overridden, and private clientelism forbidden; citizens bow the knee to nobody. And, in principle at least, republican liberty goes with democratic self-government and state accountability. In the public domain, citizens collectively define what the public interest is to be, through struggle, argument, debate and negotiation. If the rulers of the state and the officials who serve them are not accountable to the citizenry and their representatives, the language of the public interest can become a cloak for private interests. That was the moral of the Scott Report. The public interest is not a fixed essence to be derived from first principles through some allegedly value-free calculus of individual costs and benefits, or a kind of Mosaic tablet brought down from Mount Sinai by the great and good. It is inherently contestable, both in the sense that agreement on it can never be final, and in the sense that it is normally defined through conflict and the resolution of conflict.

By the same token, the public domain and its institutions and practices – at any rate in modern societies – are the sources of public trust. As wise economic liberals have always known, markets cannot work properly without trust. Nor, of course, can governments. But the market domain *consumes* trust; it does not produce it. Market actors have to trust each other. If they don't or can't, there is no market; there are only pirates or gangsters, preying on the weak and unwary. In a trustless society, exorbitant transaction costs would make market exchanges unfeasible. Trust can, of course, be produced in the private domain, and in small, face-to-face societies the trust relationships of the private domain may keep transaction costs low enough for markets to emerge. But private trust relationships are, by definition, narrow and introverted. Close-knit Peak District villages, where you are not accepted unless at least one of your grand-parents is buried in the churchyard, are not apt to trust strangers. Once market relationships extend beyond the narrow confines of a face-to-face community, public trust is indispensable to them. And public trust, like the public domain itself, is an artefact. It is a by-product of the argument and debate which are part and parcel of the public domain, and of the institutions that embody and transmit its values: an epiphenomenon of the *practice* of citizenship. For in the public domain – at least if it is working as it should – market rationality is transcended by another kind of rationality: by a civic rationality which induces trust through a complex process of social learning. But the learning process does not occur spontaneously. It depends on the institutions of the public domain and on the constraints they impose. The rule of law, enforceable contracts, enforceable property rights, and an efficient fraud squad – these quintessential products of the public domain are the bedrock of the market economy. They make it possible for market actors to learn to trust each other after all. And what is true of trust in the market-place is true more generally. Citizens trust each other because, and to the extent that, they are citizens: because, and to the extent that, they know that public institutions are governed by an ethic of equity and service. If that ceases to be true, if the public domain is invaded by the market or private domain, if justice is on sale, or public offices go to kinsfolk or croneys, trust and citizenship are both undermined.

The public domain is vulnerable as well as precious. The trust it engenders can be betrayed; and betrayal can produce a downward spiral of self-reinforcing distrust. That is what happened when ministers and officials gave misleading answers to Members of Parliament during the Arms to Iraq affair and embarked on a campaign of public sedation during the BSE crisis. The barriers that protect the public domain from invasion by the adjacent private and market domains are easily breached. Nepotism and favouritism can never be banished altogether. It is almost a law of sociology

34

that elites try to reproduce themselves; the elites of the public domain are no exception. Behind the arras encircling the public space of democratic politics lurk the loyalties of family and clan. Market power is even harder to banish. The 'universal pander of money', as Michael Walzer has hauntingly called it, sees to that.[23] Lloyd George, the pioneer of the social-citizenship state, sold honours; accusations of 'sleaze' haunted the Major Government, and now haunt the Blair Government. Much more insidious than the outright purchase of favours is the inevitable impact of private economic interests on public policy making. The DTI's excessive tenderness to the arms industry and MAFF's excessive tenderness to the livestock industry are only two cases of many. Throughout modern British history, the Treasury has displayed excessive tenderness to the financial services industry; and in the saga of the London Underground it was excessively tender to the private-sector infracos and the lawyers and consultants who advised them. There is, in fact, an inescapable tension between the egalitarian promise of democratic citizenship and the inegalitarian realities of the market domain. The capitalist renaissance of our day has made it more acute than it has been for most of the last 100 years, and exacerbated the threat it poses to the public good.

The public domain faces more subtle threats as well. It can be endangered by market mimicry, of the sort embodied in the Blair Government's PPP for the London Underground, as well as by market power. As I tried to show a moment ago, it depends, as much as anything, on an ethic or set of ethics, embodied in distinctive practices. The intrusion of market measuring rods and a market rhetoric may twist these practices out of shape, and corrode the ethics they embody and pass on. And if that happens, the motivations of the practitioners may subtly change. Instead of seeing themselves as servants of the public interest, and behaving accordingly, they may become market or quasi-market agents, maximizing their interests in a market mode, and sacrificing the public interest in the process. The introduction of performance-related pay and corporate-sector assessment procedures into the universities or the civil service may lead academics to distort their research priorities or to dilute the intellectual quality of their courses, and civil servants to become less willing to tell the truth to power. The introduction of contingency fees may lead barristers to give a lower priority to their duties to the Court and their role as upholders of the principle of equality before the law. Market-style management techniques and employment practices may lead public service broadcasters to put the pursuit of ratings ahead of public enlightenment. And when the vehicle for market mimicry is a centralized and intrusive state, in which public accountability is lacking or inadequate, all these threats may be exacerbated.

In the last two chapters of this book I shall try to show that the public domain is now under threat in precisely these ways. However, the threat can be understood only against the background of the emergence and growth of the public domain in the late nineteenth and early twentieth centuries. I turn to the complex process that enabled it to grow in the next chapter.

2

The Public Conscience

In an article in the *Nineteenth Century* in January 1887, not long after the defeat of the first Home Rule Bill, Gladstone brooded on the lessons of his long career. He drew comfort from

> a silent but more extensive and practical acknowledgement of the great second commandment, of the duties of wealth to poverty, of strength to weakness, of knowledge to ignorance, in a word of man to man. And the sum of the matter seems to be that upon the whole, and in a degree, we who lived fifty, sixty, seventy years back, and are living now, have lived into a gentler time; that the public conscience has grown more tender, as indeed was very needful; and that, in matters of practice, at sight of evils formerly regarded with indifference or even connivance, it now not only winces but rebels.[1]

Though Gladstone did not use the term, his article provides an ideal point of departure from which to explore the emergence and growth of a distinct public domain in the Victorian era – the leitmotiv of British history in the mid- and late nineteenth century and of much of his own career. Indirectly, it also throws light on the forces which lie behind its current malaise. The softening of the public conscience which he noticed had to do, above all, with a new sense of the public interest and a new willingness to assert it against the pressures of market power, on the one hand, and the ties of kinship, neighbourhood and clientelism, on the other. His 'great second commandment', with its emphasis on man's duty to man was, in essence, a commandment to put public duty and the public interest before market rewards and private interests. The malaise of the public domain in our own day reflects its loss of resonance in the final decades of the last century.

Yet the softened public conscience which delighted Gladstone did not materialize from a clear blue sky. At least two of the building blocks of the public domain constructed during the Victorian era were already in place before he entered public life. The first had to do with rhetoric, with the public philosophy, with a political ideal. Its origins went back to the civil wars of the seventeenth century, when Britain, or at least England, was the scene of a short-lived, tumult-laden, but astonishingly daring attempt to construct a self-consciously republican polity, imbued with a vision of free citizenship ultimately derived from Renaissance Italy and mediated by the Calvinist doctrine of election. The regicides called their regime a Commonwealth; the term itself implied the notion of a public domain, or *res publica*. It soon collapsed; and its apologists' attempts to discover a justification and rationale for it in a republican doctrine of civic freedom and civic duty fizzled out. But they left an enduring legacy. In the eighteenth century, the notions of the public interest, civic virtue and civic engagement were repeatedly invoked in aid by the Country Party in its struggles against the Court. So was the accompanying proposition that these were under constant threat from corruption, dependence and passivity. The ideal of civic virtue and civic duty was amorphous and inchoate. It meant different things to different people. It cut across the divisions of party and belief. But it was part of the public culture throughout the nineteenth century, and its echoes could still be heard in the first half of the twentieth.

The second building block was the law. T. H. Marshall famously argued that equality before the law was established in Britain between the Glorious Revolution of 1688 and the 1832 Reform Act, and there was justice in the claim. It would be wrong to sentimentalize the legal system of the eighteenth century. The penal code was brutal, and became more so. The law's main function was to protect property rights. Unpropertied transgressors were treated with savage cruelty. Yet in two important respects the rule of law was real, and equality before the law was real also. Social power was constrained by law; the rights of property were mediated by law; and (not least) property owners had to assert and make them effective through law. As a result, the law was a resource on which the poor and powerless, as well as the rich and powerful, could draw – albeit far less readily. The very fact that the powerful could achieve their goals only through a process of legal argument and counter-argument, carried out in public within a defined structure of inherited norms, mitigated their capacity to get their own way. As E. P. Thompson pointed out in a classic study, 'it is inherent in the especial character of law, as a body of rules and procedures, that it shall apply logical criteria with reference to standards of universality and equity'; these criteria 'perforce, had to be extended to all sorts of degrees of men'.[2] By the same token, attempts by the executive to increase its powers and curtail the liberties of the subject could be – and sometimes were – frustrated in the courts. In that sense at any rate, the great eighteenth-century jurist William Blackstone was right in thinking that Britain had a 'balanced constitution' in which an independent judiciary checked the executive.

That said, the public domain of the eighteenth century was still very narrow. The market domain was growing in vitality and importance, but the central, organizing principles of the eighteenth-century 'Old Society', as Harold Perkin calls it,[3] were those of what I have termed the private domain.

Patronage, clientelism, connection, and what a later generation would come to see as nepotism were of its essence. Loyalties were essentially familial. In many respects they had more in common with those of medieval times than with their modern successors. Eighteenth-century society was divided vertically by connection, not horizontally by class. It can best be envisaged as an interlocking nexus of familial connections: as a series of pyramids, each held together by an elaborate structure of mutual obligation running upwards and downwards, at the top of which were the members of the tiny aristocratic ruling elite. In honour – and honour was crucially important to the aristocratic code – the magnates at the top of these pyramids owed protection and patronage to those lower down. By the same token, their dependants owed them loyalty and support.

Two consequences followed, of central importance to my theme. The first is what a later generation of radical reformers were to denounce as 'Old Corruption'. In part, this was a matter of the age-old symbiosis between money and power. Places were often sinecures, sought because of the income they produced. As such, they were a form of property, to be bought and sold. 'Old Corruption' was also a matter of patronage, in today's language of nepotism. The ceaseless struggle for place, and the patronage it brought with it, was both a social necessity and a moral imperative for the aristocratic elite. It was through place and patronage that the great magnates sustained the status and power of the connections they headed, and maintained and rewarded the loyalty of the smaller fry clustered around them. All this was reflected in the ambiguous position of the Crown. Britain's was a parliamentary monarchy, not an absolute one. But the distinction between the monarch as a human person and the monarch as the embodiment of public power was still very hazy. The King was the father of his people, entitled by divine law to the obedience of his children, just as lesser fathers were entitled by the same divine law to the obedience of theirs. It does not follow that the public rhetoric of civic virtue and public duty was humbug. The statues depicting eighteenth-century statesmen in roman togas conveyed a message, as did the Latin tags that bespattered parliamentary speeches; and it was a message of senatorial dignity and public space. For all that, it embodied a myth: a myth in which the political elite believed, but still a myth.

Counter-movement

At this point Gladstone's nineteenth-century softening of the 'public conscience' comes back into the story. Though the origins of the Victorian public domain can be traced back into earlier periods, the public domain as we have known it in this country was an essentially Victorian achievement – albeit one that the twentieth century built on extensively. The great work of the Victorian era was to carve out from the encircling market and private domains a distinct, self-conscious and vigorous public domain governed by non-market and non-private norms, and to erect barriers protecting it from incursions by its market and private neighbours. The process was slow, messy and confused, but it had an under-lying logic. The richest account of that logic is still to be found in Karl Polanyi's sixty-year-old study of what he called the 'Great Transformation' from state imposed *laissez-faire* in the early decades of the nineteenth century to pragmatic, non-ideological public regulation later.[4] (His account also throws unexpected light on the dangers that face the public domain in our own day.)

Polanyi's thesis contained four crucial propositions. The supposedly self-regulating free market that emerged in Britain in the late eighteenth and early nineteenth centuries was not, he insisted, the 'natural' product of unfettered human instinct, as its apologists claimed. On the contrary, the notion of a self-regulating market was a utopian chimera It could be instantiated in a real-world society only by rooting out the values, assumptions and practices of the pre-market past.

To do this, a doctrinaire and assertive state had to force a series of brutally disruptive measures down the throat of the Old Society, much as colonial regimes had to force the subject peoples they conquered to behave in ways that accorded with classical political economy. As Polanyi put it:

> There was nothing natural about laissez-faire; free markets could never have come into being merely by allowing things to take their course. . . . laissez-faire was not a method to achieve a thing, it was the thing to be achieved. . . .
>
> The road to the free market was opened and kept open by an enormous increase in continuous, centrally organised and controlled interventionism. To make Adam Smith's 'simple and natural liberty' compatible with the needs of the human society was a most complicated affair. . . . Administrators had to be constantly on the watch to ensure the free working of the system. Thus even those who wished most ardently to free the state from all unnecessary duties, and whose whole philosophy demanded the restriction of state activities, could not but entrust the self-same state with the new powers, organs, and instruments required for the establishment of laissez-faire.[5]

However, Polanyi went on, there was a fatal flaw in the *laissez-faire* project. The self-regulating free market would work as it was supposed to work only if land, labour and money were commodified – treated as though they were commodities produced for, and bought and sold in, the market-place, like bales of cotton or sacks of coal. The labour market had to be treated like other markets. Prices (in other words, wages) had to be settled by free competition and the laws of supply and demand. The same was true of land. But, said Polanyi, labour and land are not commodities. They are not produced for the market. And if they are to be treated like commodities, an elaborate nexus of relationships, ensuring that market behaviour conforms to social norms, must be torn asunder. Labour was only 'another name for a human activity which . . . is not produced for sale but for entirely

different reasons'. Land was 'another name for nature, which
is not produced by man'. Money was a token of purchasing
power. To treat them as commodities was to fall victim to a
fiction. Yet, by a terrible irony, the fiction was fundamental
to the working of the self-regulating market.

Polanyi's third proposition followed from the second.
Because it was a utopian chimera, the self-regulating market
was by definition unfeasible. The real world could not be
forced into a free-market mould. The attempt to do so was
bound to fail. The commodification of land and labour
was bound to break down. Unfortunately, the failure did not
become apparent all at once. The fiction retained its hold on
the minds of its inventors for many decades. And so the
regime of the early nineteenth century found itself engaged in
a kind of war against social reality. The result was a disaster
– environmentally, culturally, socially and morally – that
threatened 'the demolition of society'. The commodification
of labour power stripped its human bearers of their cultural
inheritance, leaving them to perish of social dislocation. The
commodification of land produced polluted rivers, and
defiled neighbourhoods and landscapes. The commodification
of money led to periodic shortages and surfeits of purchasing
power, analogous to the floods and droughts which devastated
primitive societies.

Somehow society had to protect itself; and Polanyi's fourth
proposition is that this is precisely what happened. In
reaction to the social and cultural disaster brought about by
the *laissez-faire* utopians, and in order to save itself from
destruction, society took countervailing action. An unplanned,
un-ideological counter-movement against the imperatives of
the self-regulating market gradually gathered impetus. It was
a paradoxical affair, this counter-movement. 'Laissez-faire
was planned; planning was not. . . . The legislative spearhead
of the counter movement against a self-regulating market
as it developed in the half century following 1860 turned out
to be spontaneous, undirected by opinion, and actuated by
a purely pragmatic spirit.'[6] Examples varied from an Act

providing for the inspection of gas works to an Act making it illegal to operate a coal-mine with only a single shaft; from the Public Libraries Act that gave local authorities power, as the ultra-liberal Herbert Spencer put it, to enable a majority to tax a minority for their books; to the Workmen's Compensation Act, making employers liable for damage done to their workmen in the course of their employment.

Mastering Markets

Polanyi must not be taken neat. Ideological beliefs, moral values, cultural shifts and political leadership – indeed, conscious and deliberate human agency of any sort – play virtually no part in his explanatory scheme. The credit for the transformation from doctrinaire marketization to pragmatic regulation is given to a reified society with a capital 'S', treated almost as if it was an actor in its own right. That notion now seems curiously thin and over-simplified. The market utopianism that Polanyi attacked was part and parcel of an extraordinarily powerful and coherent ideological system (more powerful and more coherent than Polanyi's generation could easily appreciate). 'Objective' facts alone could not have prevailed against it without a change in the public philosophy. Of course, that change reflected changes in the way in which the facts were interpreted. But this is only to say that, as always, facts were mediated by beliefs. There were fierce arguments and conflicts throughout, both over marketization and over regulation. Gladstone's public conscience was always a crucial factor; and the public conscience was shaped and reshaped through moral and ideological argument and political conflict.

What this means, however, is that Gladstone and Polanyi should be put together. Their accounts are different sides of the same coin. In the jargon of social science, Gladstone focused on agency, Polanyi on structure. A full account needs both. And Polanyi was triumphantly right over certain key points – some of them as relevant to the twenty-first century as to his own day or to the period about which he was writing. The first and most important is his central proposition: that the self-regulating market order which the *laissez-faire* theorists postulated, and their political followers tried to bring into being, was a chimera. No market is ever self-regulating. Markets are embedded in society and regulated by the norms and customs of the society concerned, even if not directly and overtly by public power. There is always a moral economy: a set of norms which tell market actors how they ought to behave. By the same token, markets are political constructs. The questions are always: who does the regulating? for what purpose? in whose interests? These questions are quintessentially and inescapably political. The vogue for de-regulation which helps to explain MAFF's failures during the BSE crisis was not, as its advocates claimed, a value-free deduction from axiomatic economic truths. It was the product of a political ideology, and it served political purposes. The same is true of Labour's assumption that a public–private partnership was, by definition, the most efficient mechanism for securing adequate infrastructure investment in the London Underground. Equally resonant is Polanyi's insistence that the fundamental error of the free-market utopians was to conceive of the 'economy' – of the domain of the market – as a separate entity, conceptually distinct from society. Closely related to that error was the disastrous belief that society had to adapt to the imperatives of the market: that the market had to drive society, not society the market. Here, above all, Polanyi's thesis goes to the heart of the debate about the public domain, not only in the nineteenth and twentieth centuries, but also in the twenty-first. In this perspective, the public domain is the instrument through which market imperatives are made subordinate to social necessities and social priorities: the means through which markets are mastered for the public good,

Polanyi was also right in identifying the fundamental contradiction at the heart of the *laissez-faire* project: that if

labour and what he called land (our word would be 'environment') are treated like commodities, the consequences will be
disastrous; that the self-regulating market of *laissez-faire* theory
eats up the moral, cultural, social, human and environmental
capital on which the market order, as well as the public
domain, depends. In broad outline, he was right about the
nature of the disaster to which this experiment led. Finally,
he was right that a counter-movement took shape, fuelled by
a growing realization that the human, social and environmental damage done by marketization earlier in the century
had to be remedied, and that this could be done only if the
norms of the market-place were trumped by other norms.

The Demise of 'Old Corruption'

Against this background, the confusions and complexities
that marked the emergence of a distinct, autonomous public
domain during the Victorian era fall into place. Two
overarching themes stand out – the reconstruction of the state
and the narrowing of the market. Slowly, gradually, and with
occasional backward glances, Gladstone and his contempor-
aries dismantled the ancient structure of 'Old Corruption',
and asserted the values of citizenship, equity and service
against the clinging embrace of connection and patronage.
Their achievement was incomplete: honours were sold as
flagrantly in the early twentieth century as votes had been in
the early nineteenth. Yet they were much more successful
than their counterparts in the United States or in much of
continental Europe. By the end of the nineteenth century, the
patronage-ridden, nepotistic state of 100 years before had
been effectively replaced by an efficient, 'rational' and mod-
ernizing state, equipped with a remarkably corruption-free
Parliament and a bureaucracy recruited and promoted on
merit. Successive Reform Acts had widened the circle of
political citizenship to embrace around 60 per cent of the
adult male population, as against 9 per cent before the process

46

started. The 1872 Ballot Act and the 1884 Corrupt Practices Act had struck further blows against intimidation and vote buying. The royal prerogative had been effectively transferred from the monarch to the Government of the day. The establishment of the House of Commons Public Accounts Committee had helped to ensure that public money was properly spent; the abolition of the purchase of commissions in the army had helped to professionalize the officer corps; and the revolution in public administration that followed the 1854 Northcote–Trevelyan Report on the organization of the civil service had professionalized the higher levels of the state bureaucracy.

Four aspects of this story deserve particular attention. The first concerns the Northcote–Trevelyan Report itself. Its authors sought a disinterested, non-partisan bureaucracy, recruited on merit and consisting of generalists, formed by a broad, yet rigorous education in the humanities, rather than of narrow specialists. It was fundamental to the whole project that an overwhelming majority of these generalists would be products of the ancient universities where the political elite was itself largely formed. The higher civil service was to become a profession, but a profession of a very special kind. Recruitment on merit by open examination would ensure intellectual capacity and independence of mind; a humane education at the ancient universities would ensure a commitment to the public good. The members of this new profession would be specialists in public administration, but they would be much more than that. In effect, they were to be the guardians of the public domain; their task was not just to serve power, but to tell the truth to it. In the words of the report, they would possess 'sufficient independence, character, ability and experience to be able to advise, assist, *and to some extent influence*' the ministers in charge of their departments.[7]

Gladstone was a prime mover in the administrative revolution procured by the Report; and for Gladstone, as H. C. G. Matthew puts it, the object of the exercise was to achieve the ascendancy of a Coleridgean clerisy in the secular world. The almost absolute distinction between the administrative grade and the rest of the service, with admission to the administrative grade via examinations which were effectively a repeat of the Oxford and Cambridge degree examinations, would tend 'to strengthen and multiply the ties between the higher classes and the possession of administrative power'. A civil service hitherto appointed by patronage and influence would give way to a non-political administrative class educated in the moral values of a liberal education further developed by a reformed Oxford and Cambridge. It was a means of extending, confirming, cleansing, and legitimising an existing elite. Whereas, Gladstone thought, the seventeenth century had been an age of rule by prerogative, and the eighteenth by patronage, the nineteenth would become a rule by virtue. For a liberal education attempted, above all, to produce citizens who were morally good, and such it was that would succeed in the examinations.[8]

Rule by virtue did not mean rule by the people. The reforms that dismantled 'Old Corruption' were not intended to make Britain a democracy, and they did not do so. The suffrage was widened substantially, and attempts were made to root out bribery and intimidation, but the new voters were supposed to come only from the sections of the working class and lower middle class which possessed the moral qualities and economic independence necessary for self-reliant, active and independent citizenship. The so-called residuum of the hopeless, helpless, poverty-stricken and feckless, who were thought to be incapable of fulfilling the duties of citizenship, were not to be included in the political nation. The suffrage was not a right. It was a certificate of civic virtue or potential virtue – not just in the eyes of the existing political elite but for working-class radicals as well. As late as 1918, when manhood suffrage and limited female suffrage finally came to Britain, the Government's rationale for the change was essentially the same: that the newly enfranchised deserved full citizenship as a reward for wartime sacrifices.

By the same token, the demise of Old Corruption was not intended to create anything remotely resembling a welfare or even an interventionist state. The Gladstonian state was to be efficient, powerful and, in a sense, monarchical. The ministers at the head of it would dispose of virtually all the prerogative powers which had once belonged to the monarch. But it was also to be neutral, even aloof. It was to be free of corrupting ties to economic interests of any sort, and therefore able to take a dispassionate view of the public interest and to pursue it vigorously without fear or favour. It would hold the ring for free competition, undistorted by protection-generated monopoly, maximizing prosperity for all. But a neutral state did not imply a feeble public domain. Here the distinction between the public domain and the public sector is of crucial importance. The disinterested and powerful state that Gladstone dreamed of would hold the ring for private philanthropy as well as for free competition. Complementing it would be 'a vast network of voluntary organisations' animated by active citizens, involved in local affairs and in charitable organizations of all sorts.[9] It would lie at the heart of a lively and greatly extended public domain, whose vigour would be all the greater because it stemmed from the moral commitments of an engaged citizenry, not from state direction.

Yet there was a paradox here, which Gladstone and his fellow reformers could not have been expected to spot. As George Bernard Shaw pointed out in his contribution to the 1889 Fabian essays, the powerful, efficient, corruption-free Gladstonian state was perfectly equipped to become an instrument of collectivist interventionism – something the corrupt and patronage-encumbered state of the past could never have done. And in the twentieth century, it became just that, with huge consequences for the public domain. The disinterested, non-interventionist state became a disinterested interventionist state. The professional experts in limited government became experts in extended government.

The Moral Economy Transformed

While the assault on Old Corruption pushed back the frontiers of the private domain, a more complex set of developments did the same to the market domain. The softening of the public conscience described in Gladstone's *Nineteenth Century* article slowly transformed the moral economy. The human and social consequences of the *laissez-faire* experiment of the early century became increasingly abhorrent to enlightened people. (This is what Gladstone meant when he said that ills which had formerly been connived at now seemed intolerable.) Partly as cause and partly as consequence, there was a growing awareness that, in a range of crucial areas, the self-regulating free market did not, and could not, serve the public interest: that critically important public goods, ranging from cholera-free cities to a literate work-force, and from uplifting public spaces to food that was safe to eat, could be supplied only through public intervention, private philanthropy and/or professional commitment and expertise. The most obvious result was the slow emergence of a regulatory state. Its manifestations included the Factory Acts, the Public Health Acts, the Alkali Act, the 1872 Food and Drugs Act, and the 1875 Artisans Dwellings Act enjoining local authorities to appoint medical officers and sanitary inspectors. In essence, most of these had to do with risk management. They reflected the discovery that the new social risks created by industrialization could not be handled either through the market or through the old familial eighteenth-century order, which had, in any case, irrevocably disappeared. In Polanyesque terms, they were the products of a growing realization that the attempted commodification of land was bound to have disastrous consequences: that the self-regulating market had, and could have, no mechanism for cleaning up its own refuse, and that the state therefore had to step in. Meanwhile, more positive forms of state intervention began to remedy the damage which marketization had done to human capital. The 1870 Education Act and its later successors are the most obvious examples. Others include state regulation of working hours – a serious derogation from the free-market doctrine that the labour market is a market like any other – and legislation facilitating trade-union activity. In Polanyesque language, measures like these stemmed from the discovery that the commodification of labour was as destructive as the commodification of land.

The emergence of a regulatory state went hand in hand with a remarkable growth in private philanthropy. As Frank Prokashka puts it, 'charity saturated people's lives'. The Rothschild buildings in the East End could boast, among others, a Jews' lying-in charity, an Israelite widows' society, the Whitechapel children's care committee, a boot club, a clothing club, a children's penny dinner society, a ragged schools' union, a barefoot mission, and a savings bank run by St Jude's School.[10] Better-known charities included the Charity Organization Society, Toynbee Hall, the NSPCC, the RSPCA, the Peabody Trust, the voluntary hospitals (most of which developed in the nineteenth century), the Mother's Union and the Salvation Army. The Mother's Union had 435,000 members during the First World War. By 1893, 20,000 women – excluding nurses and women in religious orders – worked as full-time paid officials in charities. Altogether around 500,000 women worked 'continuously and semi-professionally' as volunteers in philanthropic institutions by the end of the century. Only domestic service recruited larger numbers of females. Of course, the upsurge in philanthropy did not imply a conscious backlash against free-market dogmatism. The fact remains that the charitable sector belonged unmistakably to the public domain, and not to the market domain. Charities followed non-market norms, and promoted the public interest as they saw it. Those who were active in charitable organizations were so out of a sense of duty.

Closely allied to the growth of philanthropy was the emergence of what came to be known as gas-and-water socialism

– in other words, of a vigorous form of quasi-collectivism on the local level, pursued by elected local authorities, particularly in the great industrial cities of the North and the Midlands. For the Gladstonian vision of the neutral state applied only to the national level. Local authorities in cities like Leeds, Sheffield, Liverpool, Manchester and, above all, Birmingham were far from neutral. The raw, bleak, germ-infested industrial settlements of the early nineteenth century, the Manchester of Engels and the Coketown of Dickens, became centres of civic pride, civic activism and civic enterprise. Of course, the pattern varied from authority to authority. Some cities were more energetic than others. That said, city governments in the second half of the nineteenth century cleared slums, drove new thoroughfares through noisome back alleys, established free public libraries, created public parks, built magnificent town halls mimicking Gothic cathedrals or Renaissance palazzi, and, in many cases, took gas works and water works into municipal ownership.

Joseph Chamberlain, mayor of Birmingham from 1873 to 1876, was the most famous and energetic exponent of this kind of civic activism. It was on his reputation as the chief proponent of what came to be known as the civic gospel of Birmingham that he launched his astonishing career in national politics. His own interpretation of his role as civic entrepreneur is therefore of great interest. Looking back on his Birmingham mayoralty in 1892, he wrote that the central principle of the British system of municipal government was that of a 'joint stock or co-operative enterprise in which every citizen is a shareholder, and of which the dividends are received in the improved health and the increase in the comfort and happiness of the community. . . . In no other undertaking, whether philanthropic or commercial, are the returns more speedy, more manifest, or more beneficial.'[11] It was an intriguing comment, showing that the expansion of the public domain stemmed from a 'hard', social-imperialist view of the public interest, as well as from the softer social-liberal or social-democratic view more frequently associated with it.

But Chamberlain was not the only exponent of the Birmingham gospel. Another was Robert William Dale, pastor of the Carslane Congregational Church from 1854 to 1895. Here is Dale on the new mood that began to develop in the city towards the end of the 1860s. Ward meetings, he wrote,

> assumed a new character. The speakers, instead of discussing small questions of administration and economy, dwelt with glowing enthusiasm on what a great and prosperous town like Birmingham might do for its people. They spoke of sweeping away streets in which it was not possible to live a healthy and decent life; of making the town cleaner, sweeter and brighter; of providing gardens and parks and museums; they insisted that great monopolies like the gas and water supply should be in the hands of the corporation; that good water should be supplied without stint at the lowest possible prices; that the profits of the gas supply should relieve the pressure of the rates. Sometimes an adventurous orator would excite his audience by dwelling on the glories of Florence, and of the other cities of Italy in the Middle Ages, and suggest that Birmingham too might become the home of a noble literature and art.[12]

Buttressing – and to some extent stimulating – all of this was a remarkable upsurge of organized professions, and the gradual emergence of a distinct professional class that espoused an ethic of its own.[13] In 1800 there were only seven qualifying professional associations. Between 1800 and 1880 another twenty were added to the list, embracing, among others, solicitors, architects, pharmacists, vets, surveyors, accountants and eight sorts of engineers. Between 1880 and 1914 another thirty-nine joined their number. By 1911 professionals comprised 4.1 per cent of the occupied population. If managers and administrators are added, the proportion rises to 7.5 per cent. The public domain as it developed and grew in the nineteenth and twentieth centuries was quintessentially the domain of these professionals. Professional pride, professional competence, professional duty, professional authority and, not least, predictable professional career paths were of its essence. Professionals were the chief advocates of its growth; they managed most of its institutions, and they policed the frontier between it and the adjacent private and market domains. Above all, the values of the public domain were their values. In his inaugural lecture as Professor of Political Economy at Cambridge, Alfred Marshall declared that his 'highest endeavour' would be

> to increase the numbers of those whom Cambridge, the mother of strong men, sends out into the world with cool heads and warm hearts willing to give at least some of their best powers to grappling with the social suffering around them; resolved not to rest content until they have done what in them lies to discover how far it is possible to open up to all the material means for a refined and noble life.[14]

Marshall's ambition epitomized the professional ideal. It also epitomized the cultural shift that lay behind the growth of the public domain.

To be sure, the relationship between the growth of the professions and the expansion of the public domain was far from straightforward. Marshall, after all, was no enemy to market economics; and in the nineteenth century virtually all professionals earned their living by selling their services to clients. Yet, if they were, in some sense, market traders, they were market traders of a very odd, even subversive, kind. Through their education, they had imbibed much of the aristocratic ethos of the old landed class. It was crucial to their self-esteem that they were not engaged in trade, and crucial to their interpretation of professionalism that their working practices gave them a degree of autonomy to which even the most successful market traders could not aspire. Much more important, however, was the inescapable nature of professional activity as such – above all, the special nature of the relationship between the professional and his or her clients. The market satisfies wants; professionals deal in needs. A fundamental principle of the market place is *caveat emptor* – let the buyer beware. In a professional relationship the buyer cannot beware. He has to put himself in the hands of the professional. He cannot himself judge the quality of the service, or not, at any rate, until it is too late. When the layman consults a professional, as T. H. Marshall pointed out, 'Authority passes from buyer to seller. . . . When the doctor says, "Take more exercise", it is a command. When the associated greengrocers plaster the hoardings with the slogan, "Eat more fruit", it is an effort at mass suggestion.'[15]

It follows that the professional must possess properly certified qualifications. The client cannot assess the validity of these qualifications, but she can know whether or not the professional possesses them. She puts her fate in the hands of the professional only because she believes that the professional possesses the relevant expertise – hence, the crucial importance of the qualifying association. The professional association certifies that its members do indeed possess the necessary expertise. That, in turn, implies control of entry into the profession. And what this means is that the professional ethic encodes an implicit bargain between professionals and the wider society. Professionals are allowed to restrict entry and, at least to a degree, to fix prices – in other words, to command a rent over and above what strict adherence to the market norms of free competition would yield them – and in return they are expected to internalize a set of norms precluding them from abusing their monopoly position and exploiting their clients, and enjoining them to promote the public good. This, in turn, means that professionalism is, in a profound sense, not just non-market but anti-market. At the heart of the bargain between the professional and the wider society lies the premiss that society will be better off if, in the particular sphere where the professional operates, market norms are suspended. Where the fundamental assumption of the market domain is that wealth will be maximized, and the greatest good of the greatest number achieved, if resources flow in the direction dictated by free competition, the professional ethic asserts the contrary. It presupposes that, in the particular case of the market for a special category of highly qualified manpower, competition should not be free; that entry ought to be controlled; that prices ought to be fixed; that monopoly rents, or at any rate the processes of certification and validation which produce monopoly rents, are in the public interest.

Implications

The early twentieth century saw further portentous changes in the political and moral economies. The size and scope of the state increased dramatically. Public expenditure, which accounted for 13.3 per cent of GDP in 1900, accounted for 24.5 per cent in 1937. The Education Act of 1902, the introduction of Old Age Pensions in 1908, and the National Insurance Act of 1911 laid the foundations of the welfare state completed by the wartime coalition of 1940–5 and the Labour governments of 1945–51. Bitter industrial unrest immediately before and after the First World War, culminating in the doomed General Strike of 1926, led eventually to a tacit settlement between organized labour and organized capital, blessed, and to some extent cemented, by the state. The professions, which had spearheaded the growth of the public domain in the second half of the nineteenth century, became even more sizeable, more numerous and more confident. The climate of opinion changed *pari passu. Laissez-faire* utopianism did not die out altogether, but it was in universal retreat. The common sense of the 1930s was for state intervention in the economy and a gradual extension of collective provision in social policy. The only questions were how far these should go, and what form they should take. However, these changes did not mark a break with those of the late nineteenth century. The public domain of the inter-war years was bigger than that of the 1880s and 1890s, but the logic of its growth was unchanged.

The implications of this complex story go wide. Plainly, the public domain grew in response to 'objective' factors – in particular, to the increasingly apparent need to manage the social risks associated with industrialization and urbanization, and to the associated need to incorporate the increasingly class-conscious labour movement into the political order. This growth also had a dynamic of its own. Once small breaches were made in the dykes of the self-regulating market order, bigger breaches followed almost inexorably. The successive Public Health Acts are good cases in point. But that is only part of the story. The values that sustain, and are in turn sustained by, the public domain – the values of professionalism, citizenship and service – are, historically speaking, rare breeds. In the public domain, to take only a couple of obvious examples, parents are supposed to subordinate the interests of their children to a remote public interest. Monetary rewards are supposed to count for less than the sense that a job has been well done. In most cultures at most times, such behaviour and the attitudes that sustain it would have seemed (and in many still seem) cold, hard, impersonal, even a little inhuman. The social benevolence engendered in the public domain is an austere, slightly distant benevolence. Its values run counter to the familial loyalties and patronage linkages characteristic of pre-modern societies. They imply a certain discipline, a certain self-restraint, which do not come naturally, and have to be learned and then internalized, sometimes painfully. Their installation in a real-world society requires a cultural and ideological revolution.

Revolutions are almost always the work of elites, and the ideological and cultural revolution that sowed the values of the public domain in the originally inhospitable soil of nineteenth-century Britain was no exception. It too was the work of elites confident of their legitimacy and proud of their status. Some of them belonged to the so-called labour aristocracy which campaigned for parliamentary reform and ran the co-operative societies, friendly societies and craft unions of late Victorian Britain. But in Britain, at any rate, the growth of the public domain owed most to the self-consciously professional elites discussed above. Yet its growth cannot be understood as the straightforward product of a social interest. Doctrine, values, ideas, *ideologies* played a crucial role. To be sure, the ideologies of the public domain formed a confused medley. Different discourses criss-cross in a rich, but confusing fashion. Leading contributors to them include such diverse figures as John Stuart Mill, particularly in the later editions of his *Political Economy*; the economist Alfred Marshall; the social liberals J. A. Hobson and Leonard Hobhouse; the unclassifiable, quicksilver-minded John Maynard Keynes; and the social democrats R. H. Tawney, Evan Durbin, Richard Titmuss and Anthony Crosland. As I mentioned a moment ago, the right of the political spectrum also contributed significantly. Joseph Chamberlain has already been mentioned in this connection, and the young Harold Macmillan also deserves a place in the pantheon. So, it goes without saying, does Gladstone. For Gladstone staked his whole career on the propositions that there is a public interest which goes wider than the sum of private interests; that it can and should be determined through a process of debate and argument; and that, by appealing to their better natures, the public can be mobilized behind a legislative programme and a series of executive actions designed to pursue it. It is not irrelevant that one of the main reasons why the later Gladstone came to believe that the masses were better citizens than the classes is that he also came to believe that they were more willing to subordinate narrow, selfish concerns to the public good.

Certain themes, however, sound through the medley. First and foremost comes the notion of active citizenship, inherited, no doubt, from the Country Party polemicists of the eighteenth century, and more distantly from the Commonwealth theorists of the seventeenth. The notion was complex and subtle. Crucial to it was the assumption that it was possible for free men to engage in disinterested reflection, and to exercise independent, unbiased judgement on the issues of the day. For Mill, politics was essentially a form of social discovery or mutual education; and he spoke for many. This implied, among other things, that political preferences are not fixed; that they can be altered by moral persuasion and free debate; and that the task of political leaders is to do just that. In sharp contrast to market exchanges, politics is a process not of registering preferences but of changing them. That was the leitmotiv of Gladstone's Midlothian campaign and of his doomed battle for Irish Home Rule.

In the later decades of the nineteenth century and at the beginning of the twentieth, a cross-cutting theme also appeared. Thanks, above all, to Darwinian biology, the organic metaphor of society became increasingly prevalent. A range of implications followed. The most obvious was that society is quintessentially interdependent. Another was that the health of the social organism should be the central preoccupation of the statesman. Damage to the health of one part of the organism would damage the whole. Poverty, malnutrition, disease, even unemployment may afflict only a section of society, but in afflicting that section, they afflict the entire society. That is one of the reasons why the notion of need also played such a crucial role in the debates that fostered the public domain. Medical intervention is necessary to cure a sick organism; and it is the task of medical science to determine whether or not the organism needs intervention. The opinions of the putative beneficiaries hardly count: patients are not supposed to diagnose themselves. Notoriously, the working classes were initially suspicious of the movement towards a welfare state which gathered momentum in the period before the First World War, largely because they saw the state as an enemy rather than a friend. But for the advocates of the measures concerned, that was almost irrelevant. The point of the 1911 National Insurance Act providing, for the first time, an embryonic form of social insurance against sickness and unemployment, was not to please the working classes; it was to cure a sickness of the social whole.

Closely related to all this was a growing concern with uncertainty, with risk and with the need for collective insurance against it. That was the rationale for the National Insurance Act, for its extensions in the inter-war period and for the Beveridgean welfare state established by the post-war Labour Government. Social risk was one of the main preoccupations of Richard Titmuss, and it played a central role in the economic doctrines that John Maynard Keynes hammered out in the 1920s and 1930s. For Keynes, the fact that we live in a world of uncertainty and risk, where money is both a store of value and a medium of exchange, leads inexorably to the conclusion that supply and demand will normally balance at less than full employment. That, in turn, leads to the conclusion that only a new and permanent form of macro-economic management can ensure that they balance at full employment instead. Like Beveridge, Keynes proposed a form of collective risk management, designed to procure a public good which markets could not supply. Here need comes back into the story once again, closely related to time. For the theorists of the public domain, social needs are to take precedence over market wants; the long-term health of the social organism is to be prioritized over the satisfaction of short-term wants through the market mechanism. A further implication follows as well. Without putting it in this way, the champions of the emerging public domain were seeking to re-embed the economy in society: to create new links binding market and society into a composite whole, in place of the old links which had been smashed at the beginning of the century.

There was a worm in the bud. As I tried to show in the last chapter, accountability in the market domain comes through Exit and the threat of Exit. That is how producers are made accountable to consumers, and how consumers ensure that they are not exploited by market power or vested interests. In the public domain, however, accountability through Exit is, by definition, not available. The relationships of the public domain are necessarily long-term. The loyalties which are fundamental to it could not take root in, and would not survive, a regime of Exit. It follows that, in the public domain, accountability can come only through Voice – in other words through argument, discussion, debate and democratic engagement. But in nineteenth- and early-twentieth-century Britain, accountability through Voice was lacking or attenuated; and the growth of the public domain did nothing to enhance it. As I tried to show a moment ago, the Gladstonian central state was not supposed to be democratic, still less participatory: it was not Robert Dale's Birmingham ward meeting writ large, and few members of the political class would have wished it to be. At its core lay a tradition of autonomous executive power, going back to the eighteenth century, and perhaps even to royalist apologists at the start of the English Civil War. In 1900, no less than in 1800 or 1700, Britain's was a parliamentary *monarchy*, and both words in that phrase count equally.

The monarch's prerogative powers had passed to the Queen's ministers, not to Parliament or the people; and they were still essentially monarchical in character. The Northcote–Trevelyan-inspired reforms of public administration were explicitly intended to reserve the highest posts in the new, patronage-free bureaucracy to a small elite drawn overwhelmingly from the two ancient universities. Despite his deepening faith in the civic potential of the masses, Gladstone was, in this sense, a quintessential Whig, whose purpose was to repair and even, if necessary, to reconstruct an ancient building, not to build a new one. The new, reformed state was a cleaned-up version of the old state. The new groups admitted to the franchise were admitted only because it was assumed that they had the capacity to be socialized into the values and mores of the existing regime. With only a handful of exceptions, the new men who arrived little by little in the House of Commons were indeed socialized into them. And if this was true of the political culture, it was equally true of the wider public culture, and not least of the professional culture that the professional ethic encapsulated. Professionals served the public, and pursued what they believed to be the public interest; but they were accountable only to their fellow professionals. It took a long time for the worm to make its presence felt. The process through which it did so will be one of the central themes of the next chapter.

3

Troubled Zenith

By the middle of the twentieth century, the public domain had reached its zenith. Gladstone's tender public conscience had extended its frontiers far more widely than he could have foreseen or would have wished. Polanyi's counter-movement against the *laissez-faire* utopianism of the early nineteenth century seemed universally victorious. After listing the welfare services provided by the central state, an official handbook, published by His Majesty's Stationery Office in 1949, observed with pardonable complacency: 'None of these services has been imposed by the State on an unwilling public. All of them are the result of cooperative effort between successive governments and the people whom they governed.'[1] Few would have dissented. The welfare state, whose foundations had been laid by the Liberal Government before 1914, had been consolidated along the lines put forward by William Beveridge in his famous 1942 report. The proposition that only the state could provide adequate collective insurance against ill health, unemployment and the hazards of old age was part of the common sense of the age. Beveridgean social citizenship went hand in hand with a new kind of economic citizenship. It was taken for granted that continuous macro-economic regulation on Keynesian lines could and should safeguard society against the risk of recurrent bouts of high unemployment: that full employment should be seen as a public good which it was the duty of the state to provide.

The Beveridgean and Keynesian revolutions were epiphenomena of a more profound revolution in the moral economy and public culture. The old, eighteenth-century notion of absolute property had gradually given way to a fuzzy, ill-defined, but nevertheless pervasive conception of property as a social trust. One manifestation was a deliberately redistributive system of direct taxation. By the end of the Second World War the standard rate of income tax was 10 shillings in the pound (i.e. 50 per cent), while the highest marginal rate had reached 97.5 per cent. Another was the emergence of what came to be known as a mixed economy – in other words, an economy with a substantial (though not predominant) publicly owned sector. To be sure, its rationale was confused, to say the least. For social-democratic thinkers like Evan Durbin, and for the official Labour Party in its 1945 election platform, public ownership was a means to the greater end of a socially controlled economy animated by public purpose, expressed in a rational and comprehensive plan, rather than by private profit seeking. Events made nonsense of the social-democratic vision. The 1945 Government soon discovered that economic planning as envisaged in the 1945 manifesto was unfeasible, at any rate for a Government that depended heavily on the trade unions and was therefore unable to plan wages, and in an economy dependent on the inherently unplannable vagaries of foreign trade.

However, the social-democratic case for public ownership ran alongside a technocratic case, reflecting the particular needs and interests of the candidates for nationalization, to which overt party doctrine was almost irrelevant; and the technocratic case turned out to be much more robust. The Attlee Government's nationalization measures transferred more than two million workers from the private to the public sector; more than £2,500 million was paid out in compensation. Yet there was serious controversy only over steel. Looked at through the prism of social-democratic ideology, nationalization was a sad disappointment. The nationalized industries did not become agents of a purposive state; nor did they make it easier to plan the economy. Yet their very existence carried a message whose full significance did not become apparent until the wave of privatization that swept across the economic landscape in the 1980s. Private property rights were no longer sacrosanct. By implication, at least, private owners had public duties. If they failed to discharge them, they might be expropriated.

In practice, no such message was necessary. Big private firms did not behave very differently from their public-sector counterparts. They were run, for the most part, by the same sorts of people in the same sort of way. Swashbuckling private-sector buccaneers were still to be found here and there, but they were a rare breed. The risk-taking owner-manager of the first Industrial Revolution, who raised his own capital, hired his own labour, found his own markets, and faced personal ruin if his decisions turned out to be wrong, was virtually extinct. Like nationalized industries, or for that matter Government departments, big privately owned firms were organized hierarchically and run by salaried professionals. They still had to meet the tests of the market-place, but its rigours were much less fierce than they had been in the past. The ruthlessness of traditional capitalism had largely disappeared, Anthony Crosland argued in 1956.

> The talk, and part of it at least is genuine, is now of the social responsibilities of industry – to workers, consumers, the locality, retiring employees, disabled workers.... Aggressive individualism is giving way to a suave and sophisticated sociability: the defiant cry of 'the public be damned' to the well-staffed public relations department: the self-made autocratic tycoon to the arts graduate and the scientist: the invisible hand ... to the glad hand. Private industry is at last becoming humanised.[2]

Crosland's conclusion that capitalism had metamorphosed into something quite different was wide of the mark. The glad hand was a marketing device, not an expression of the civic ideal. But he was right in thinking that the corporate managers who dominated the commanding heights of the private sector were closer in ethos and mentality to their counterparts in the professions and the public services than to the classical entrepreneurs of 100 years before. They were subject to market imperatives, but many of them adhered to the values of the public domain as well.

Much of the credit for the 'humanisation' of the private sector went to a profound shift in the balance of industrial power. The old doctrine of absolute property rights had been symbiotically linked to the commodification of labour excoriated by Polanyi. Property owners had a right to do as they wished with their own; 'their own' included the workers they hired and fired at will. As I tried to show in the last chapter, the emerging regulatory state of the late nineteenth and early twentieth centuries had steadily chipped away at the outworks of that doctrine. Little by little, a vague, hazy, inexplicit notion of industrial citizenship began to soften the rigours of the labour market. Employers' rights were circumscribed in a host of ways; if only by implication, employees were granted countervailing rights as well. The Keynesian revolution gave the process a powerful new boost. Full employment hugely increased the bargaining power of organized labour and (perhaps even more significantly) raised the status and self-confidence of all workers, whether organized or not. The oft-repeated saying that the trade unions had become an estate of the realm was misleading. British trade unions had grown up outside the law, and they were imbued with a visceral suspicion of the common-law tradition to which the notions of collective rights and collective bargaining were alien. They sought (and obtained) immunities from legal penalties, not positive and justiciable legal protection. 'Free collective bargaining' – by which they meant collective bargaining conducted without interference by the Government or the courts – was their mantra. Attempts to turn them into corporatist social partners on central European or Scandinavian lines always foundered. Wartime regulation and post-war full employment made them far more powerful than they had been before, but their power was negative rather than positive. All the same, it was a formidable constraint on the freedom of action of the capitalist employer.

The zenith of the public domain was also the zenith of the professionalism of which it was both child and parent. Professionals headed the bureaucracies that ran the Beveridgean welfare state, and controlled the services that its beneficiaries enjoyed. Ministers manipulated the levers of Keynesian economic management in accordance with the advice of professional economists, tempered by that of professional civil servants. Professionals controlled the newly nationalized industries, while other professionals, with essentially the same qualifications, ran the big firms that dominated the private sector. The leaders of the great trade unions were also professionals of a sort; and one of their main objectives was to win their members status, job security and autonomy of the kind that professionals already enjoyed. Harold Perkin's description of the consequences could hardly be bettered. In the post-war period, he wrote,

> professional society reached a plateau of attainment. This did not mean a utopia based entirely on merit, social efficiency and social justice. It meant, rather, a society which accepted in principle that ability and expertise were the only respectable justification for recruitment to positions of authority and responsibility and in which every citizen had the right to a minimum income in times of distress, to medical treatment during sickness, to decent housing in a healthy environment, and an education appropriate to his or her abilities. . . .
>
> . . . To that extent, the professional ideal was the organizing principle of post-war society.[3]

The Civic Ideal under Pressure

Beneath the surface, however, the enlarged public domain of the mid-twentieth century was less secure than it looked. Social citizenship, economic citizenship and a tentative, embryonic form of industrial citizenship had made great advances. Political citizenship had become 'thinner' and more passive. The aloof, monarchical Gladstonian state had become incomparably bigger, but it was still aloof and still monarchical; thanks to the increased size and complexity of Government and the growth of a disciplined party system, the ministers and officials at the head of it were, in practice, less accountable to Parliament and the public than they had been seventy years before. One of the by-products of the Beveridgean and Keynesian revolutions, moreover, was a much more centralized polity and a much more powerful state. The once-vibrant local authority sector, which had been one of the drivers of the expanding public domain of the nineteenth century, now saw its wings severely clipped. The nationalization of the public utilities – electricity and gas in particular – cut heavily into the autonomy of the local authorities, which had owned substantial portions of both. Power was transferred from elected councillors, relatively close to the communities for which they spoke, to remote authorities only dubiously accountable to elected persons of any sort.

Much the same was true of the National Health Service. An emblematic moment came within a few months of the 1945 election, when Herbert Morrison and the Health Minister, Aneurin Bevan, clashed over the fate of the hospital service. Bevan wanted to nationalize the hospitals, on the grounds that an efficient hospital service could be achieved only by centralizing responsibility for it. Both the private voluntary hospitals and the municipal hospitals would therefore have to be included in a single nationalized entity. Herbert Morrison opposed nationalization, on the grounds that it would undermine local democracy. When the battle came to the Cabinet, the young and inexperienced Bevan prevailed against Herbert Morrison, then at the plenitude of his power as Deputy Prime Minister, with long years at the top of the Labour movement to his credit. Then and later, the decision was seen in the Labour movement as a victory for red-blooded socialism over pale pink pusillanimity. The truth was more complicated. Morrison was as firm in his socialist faith as Bevan was. At stake were contrasting visions of politics and the good life which cut across the familiar divisions between socialists and anti-socialists, and left and right. Bevan, the wayward rebel, was a centralist to his finger tips. What mattered was national equity, which only the central state could deliver. On many issues, Morrison was a centralist too, but in the battle over hospital nationalization he was a localist. His defeat was a defeat for localist values that privileged responsiveness to local priorities over efficiency, and self-government over uniformity. Yet in the great days of the civic ideal, these localist values had done much to give it its cutting edge. It would be wrong to depict Bevan as an enemy of the public domain, and Morrison as a friend. Both were friends. Equity is one of its fundamental values; and Bevan believed he was fighting for equity. All the same, his victory (and still more its enthusiastic reception on the left) revealed a growing tendency to sacrifice civic engagement on the altar of centrally determined efficiency. As the next chapter will show, that tendency was to bear paradoxical fruit.

For some time, deeper currents of thought and feeling had been flowing in the same direction. The inter-war years had seen a sharp break in the intellectual and cultural climate, at any rate among the avant-garde and the rebellious young. It was the age of the spare, the hard, the reductionist, the pared-down, the *mechanical* – Bauhaus architecture, Taylorism in industrial management, Pavlov and Freud in psychology, Lewis Namier in history, A. J. Ayer and the Vienna Circle in philosophy, Auden in poetry, the Soviet Five-Year Plans, and Truby King's approach to child care. The task of the intellectual and the artist was to cut through richly textured, inevitably misleading surfaces in order to expose the secret realities beneath. Hegelian idealism gave way to logical positivism, and later to linguistic analysis; moral earnestness to a hard-edged, often mocking, pretended realism. The style and content of late Victorian and Edwardian public discourse came to seem vague, empty, self-deceptive and even hypo-critical – ripe for unmasking and debunking. Lytton Strachey's 'eminent Victorians' were, at best, pompous, deluded fools; at worst, dishonest rogues. In *The Economic Consequences of the Peace*, J. M. Keynes immortalized a biting caricature of Woodrow Wilson as a foolish, bamboozled old man, too proud and stubborn to admit that he was wrong.

By the same token, the 'soft', essentially moralistic themes of pre-1914 political debate – citizenship and its obligations, the scope and nature of Britain's national identity, the reform of the Constitution, the rights and roles of women – gave way to the 'hard' themes of class conflict and economic organization. On the left, the mechanistic, state-centred collectivism of the Fabians drowned out the moralistic pluralism of the social liberals. Political reform came to seem irrelevant and old hat. What mattered was to use the power of the central state to transform society; its form and nature could be left for later. The pluralist, participatory themes of the young Harold Laski and the young G. D. H. Cole were largely forgotten – even, it sometimes seemed, by their authors. And in this, at least, the right mirrored the left. As a result, talk of citizenship in the nineteenth-century sense of the term – citizenship as a strenuous, testing collective moral enterprise that depended on a capacity for personal growth and the exercise of self-discipline – began to seem empty, self-indulgent and, worse still, quaint and old-fashioned.

Of course, it did not disappear altogether. There was much recourse to it in the Second World War. The endless exhorta-tions of the wartime state – to dig for victory, to live cleanly, to eat potatoes, to refrain from careless talk – were couched in terms of civic duty. The same was true of the Attlee

Government in the immediate post-war period. Central to Stafford Cripps's conception of democratic planning was the assumption that private economic agents had a duty to abide by the terms of a plan hammered out in a consultative process, and (still more remarkably) that that duty would be performed. Ernest Bevin based his unyielding opposition to state interference with free collective bargaining on the assumption that the bargainers could be persuaded voluntarily to pay due heed to the public interest. On another level, it is important to remember that T. H. Marshall, whose classic study *Citizenship and Social Class* was not published until 1950, worked and wrote in the civic tradition, as did Richard Titmuss, whose most important contributions appeared still later.

Namierites and Schumpeterians

Though the citizenship ideal of the nineteenth and early twentieth centuries still resonated in some quarters, however, the tides of intellectual fashion were steadily eroding the assumptions on which it was founded. Much more characteristic of the prevailing mentality than Marshall or Titmuss were the historiography of Lewis Namier and the political economy of Joseph Schumpeter. For them, the language of civic duty and civic activism was so much hot air. When the resounding rhetoric of the Country Party politicians of the eighteenth century was stripped away, said Namier, what emerged was a politics of place, connection and interest, to which ideas were irrelevant and in which language was merely a weapon in the struggle for power. For Schumpeter, the 'classical', participatory vision of democracy propounded in past centuries was humbug – and potentially dangerous humbug at that. It had, and could have, no meaning in the real world of the mid-twentieth century. For, in truth, political leaders were akin to entrepreneurs in the market-place. Whereas entrepreneurs maximized, or sought to maximize,

their profits, political leaders maximized, or sought to maximize, their votes. By the same token, voters were akin to
consumers. They shopped around for the political product that
would maximize their utility in the most cost-effective way.
The public realm ceased to be a realm of debate, of reflection,
or of persuasion. It became a special kind of market-place.
Indeed, on Schumpeterian assumptions, the very term 'public
realm' was misleading: in the polity no less than in the
economy, individual utility maximization was the sole driving
force. The suggestion that there is, or ought to be, a distinct
and autonomous public domain, observing different norms
from those of the market domain, was high-sounding cant.

Namierites and Schumpeterians purported to offer a neutral, value-free description of the way in which the political
world worked, but their visions of politics were as normative
as those they claimed to have supplanted. Despite appearances
to the contrary, they did not say merely that the political
world worked in the way that they described. If only by
implication, they also said that this was how it was bound to
work, and indeed how it ought to work: that political systems
could function properly only if the illusory expectations
engendered by the classical vision were abandoned. They were
not alone. In a classic cross-national study in 1963, Gabriel
Almond and Sydney Verba concluded that voter deference
towards the political elite was as crucial to the health and
stability of a democratic polity as participation through the
ballot-box and a willingness to influence political leaders.
Britain was the model 'civic culture', as they defined it,
because she exhibited the ideal combination of deference and
participation.[4] In a widely used American textbook on com-
parative government, also published in the early 1960s, Harry
Eckstein argued that the British Government was 'uniquely
effective' because '[v]oluntary submission to leadership is,
even today . . . a vital part of British political culture'.[5]

It is hard to believe that Namier, Schumpeter and the
behaviourist political scientists of the early 1960s had many
readers among politicians and journalists, but there is no

doubt that they reflected – and at the same time reinforced – the dominant strand in the mentality of the political class. It was best epitomized in a brilliant series of lectures by the Tory imperialist and All Souls Fellow L. S. Amery. The British Constitution, Amery argued, had always been structured around a dialogue, or 'parley', between two coequal elements – the Crown or Government, which directed and energized, and the Nation, which assented or acquiesced. That tradition of autonomous, but responsive executive power was the key to Britain's political good fortune. It followed that the nineteenth-century commentators who assumed that Parliament governed in accordance with the wishes of an active electorate had 'misread' the Constitution they thought they were expounding. In doing so, they had encouraged Britain's continental imitators to adopt a form of government which was

> bound, by its very nature, to be weak and unstable. . . . Face to face with the growing need of the age for more governmental action and more definite leadership, it has almost everywhere broken down. The rise of dictatorships and of one-party government has been the almost inevitable consequence of the ineffectiveness of constitutions which have reproduced the outward form of the British Constitution without that spirit of strong and stable government which is of its essence.[6]

The implications were startling. The great question that preoccupied the political class during the nineteenth-century debates on the suffrage was whether the disenfranchised masses possessed the moral qualities necessary for active citizenship. Now the political class had itself abandoned active citizenship for the sake of stability.

By a strange irony, however, the citizenry turned out to be closer to the allegedly mistaken commentators of the nineteenth century than to the hard-nosed realists of the mid-twentieth. Immediately after the Second World War, when Amery's lectures were delivered, public confidence in the victory-sanctified British state and its institutions was at its height. The next quarter of a century saw a dramatic change in the public mood. An attitude survey carried out for the Kilbrandon Commission on the Constitution in 1970 reported a 'diffuse feeling of dissatisfaction' with the existing system of government. Of those questioned, 49 per cent thought the system either needed 'a great deal of improvement' or 'could be improved quite a lot'. Only 5 per cent thought it worked 'extremely well'. Of those questioned, 55 per cent felt 'very powerless' or 'fairly powerless' in the face of Government; and it was among those who felt powerless that dissatisfaction was most marked. Later studies suggested that dissatisfaction was a function of distrust; and that distrust was rooted in a perceived discrepancy between the realities of politics and the proclaimed ideals of the system. The distrustful were not estranged from democratic norms. They were estranged from a system that failed to observe them.[7]

The monarchical state remained in being. The tradition of autonomous executive power which was its lodestar still prevailed in Westminster and Whitehall. But it rested on an ever-narrower basis of popular support; and dwindling legitimacy eroded the strength and stability that Amery had lauded. The governments of the 1960s all tried to halt the relative decline of the British economy through varied forms of indicative planning, and they all failed. The Wilson Government of 1966–70 was forced to devalue sterling against its will, and had to retreat ignominiously in the face of trade-union opposition to its proposed reform of industrial relations. The governments of the 1970s were all baffled by the alarming new phenomenon of 'stagflation' – a combination of rising unemployment and rising inflation that the economics profession could not understand, let alone cure – and battered by the storms that swept over the global economy following the oil shock of 1973. The Heath Government of 1970–4 was twice brought to its knees by a newly militant miners' union, while the Callaghan Government of 1976–9 was forced to seek credits from the IMF to halt a flight from the pound. By the end of the third quarter of the twentieth century, the British state was in a condition of incipient crisis. The public domain of which it was an essential custodian was more vulnerable than at any time since its Victorian emergence.

The Paradoxes of Professionalism

Professionals, professionalism and the professional ethic experienced a milder version of the same fate. The cultural shifts which had undermined the nineteenth-century citizenship ideal slowly reordered the discourse of professionalism and the self-image of the professional class. The nineteenth-century themes of service, equity and trust remained central to both, but they came to be articulated in a language of positivist rationality rather than one of civic engagement. More and more, professionals saw themselves, and (more importantly) presented themselves to the wider society, as technocratic specialists rather than members of, and contributors to, a broader civic community. To put it another way, they became increasingly prone to base their claims to professional status and professional rewards on their possession of technical skills, technical knowledge and technical qualifications which the laity did not possess, rather than on their commitment to the public good; and to base their claim to autonomy on the alleged inability of the laity to understand and assess what they did.

All too often, the result was a hubristic tunnel vision on the part of the professions and a sense of baffled unease on the part of a public whose ability to hold the professionals to account had not kept pace with their increasing hermeticism and self-confidence. The inhuman tower blocks that bespattered council estates; the urban motorways that tore the hearts out of so many provincial city centres; the uneconomic and dangerous obsession with civil nuclear power; the landscape-destroying growth of intensive agriculture were all monuments to a combination of professional hubris and professional power.

In many ways, however, the academic profession offers the most instructive example of the reordering of the professionals' view of themselves and their role. The growing prestige of the natural sciences, and the associated, almost exponential growth in scientific knowledge and the effectiveness of applied science, led academics in the humanities and, still more, in the social sciences to imitate their scientific colleagues in certain key respects. Formerly, they had seen themselves as part of a broader public culture, to whose development they were duty-bound to contribute, and which they enriched by doing so. Now they tended increasingly to turn their backs on the public culture, and on the concerns of those who inhabited it. Increasingly, historians wrote for other professional historians rather than for the general public, and were judged by their capacity to practise their craft according to the rules laid down by the historical profession. Economists increasingly saw themselves as high theorists or technical experts whose public role was confined to advising governments on how best to manipulate economic variables, rather than as architects of a better moral economy. The newer social sciences, sociology and political science in particular, followed suit. Even philosophers abandoned the terrain of moral prescription in favour of an aseptic and essentially technocratic approach, whereby their task was to clarify the use of words and to correct the fallacies that derived from their misuse. As a result, the academic profession became a secular priesthood, preoccupied by its own, increasingly arcane internal arguments, all too often expressed in a rebarbative and inaccessible jargon and developed in obscure journals whose editorial practices aped those of the natural sciences. The public culture was impoverished; and the academy cut itself off from the living forces of the outside world. A growing gulf divided the public beyond the seminary walls from the academics within them, which was to have disastrous consequences in the 1980s and 1990s.

All this gave extra edge to a destructive paradox which had always lain at the heart of the relationship between professionalism and the public domain. The public domain is, among other things, the domain of professionalism, and professionalism is inescapably elitist. Professionals can function only if they are trusted. The surgeon's skills, the scholar's learning, the judge's impartiality, the policeman's probity, the social worker's insight have to be taken on trust by those who consume the services they provide. Appraisal systems, league tables, performance indicators, and all the fashionable bric-à-brac of modern management may provide safeguards against the abuse of trust, but they operate in general terms, and after the event. At the crucial moment – discussing the pros and cons of an operation with a consultant, instructing a solicitor about a divorce settlement, telling a policeman about the circumstances of a break-in, listening to a tutor's comments on an essay – they pale into insignificance. At such moments, the client has no option but to trust the professional. To withdraw trust is to corrode the essential professional relationship, and to degrade the service which it is the professional's duty to provide. It follows that professionalism is symbiotically related to authority. For trust and authority go hand in hand. I trust a professional because, and in so far as, I accept the authority of the professional's office and the authority of those who certified her as competent to exercise her professional functions. We pay professionals for their services, and we offer them status and autonomy, because in their own field they know more than we do; and therefore we defer to them. No elites, no professions; and no public domain either.

Yet the public domain is also the domain of citizenship, and citizenship is in principle inclusive. However, the professional elites which nurture and sustain it are inevitably exclusive. They can of course be open to talent, meritocratic in their promotions procedures, and equitable in their approach to non-members; but not everyone can belong to them. An elite to which everyone belonged would not be an elite at all. The elites that peopled Britain's public domain in its great days were in the main public spirited, high-minded, even, on occasion, self-sacrificing. But they were still elites, they still excluded more people than they included, and their public spirit and high-mindedness went hand in hand with an incorrigible propensity to patronize those outside their ranks and a blithe inability to see that their impartiality and devotion to the public good might not appear self-evident to those adversely affected by their decisions. The more specialized they became, and the more vigorously they based their claim to status and autonomy on essentially technical grounds, the more uneasy they made the public. Judges, civil servants, surgeons, academics, road engineers, town planners, social workers, public-service broadcasters all insisted that they knew best – that they knew best by definition, because they had been trained to know best. In the still deeply class-divided, but in retrospect extraordinarily deferential, society of the early postwar years, their authority was generally accepted along with their claims to competence and impartiality, but by the 1970s it was beginning to be called into question. The professional, generalist civil service engendered by the Northcote–Trevelyan Report was accused of amateurishness (not least by politicians anxious to find a scapegoat for the policy failures of the time); welfare professionals were accused of putting their own interests above those of their clients; solicitors were accused of restrictive practices; academics were accused of a self-indulgent indifference to the economic and social needs of the society that paid their salaries.

Part of the explanation lay in a further paradox – the paradox of professional society. The number of professions continued to grow; professionalism steadily expanded its frontiers; and the numbers entitled to claim professional status grew *pari passu*. But there was an unexpected consequence. Professional society is, by definition, knowledge-intensive; and the more knowledge-intensive society becomes, the less deferential it is likely to be. A better-educated public will, other things being equal, be more confident of its own judgement, and less content to take authority on trust. Of course, new entrants to the professional class claimed authority and public trust for themselves: that claim was intrinsic to professional status. But they were less willing than their non-professional forbears had been to trust other professionals (even other new professionals) or to defer to their authority. The result was fragmentation, even a kind of implosion. The professional class and professional culture were not homogeneous. They were made up of a growing plethora of subcultures, each claiming its own authority and each using its own specialized language. Sometimes these subcultures were rivals, as with doctors and osteopaths. Even when they were not, there were no cross-cutting ties of interest or feeling to bind them together. Social workers sought professional authority for themselves; they did not much care what happened to barristers or estate agents. Shared professional status did not give solicitors a fellow-feeling for architects which coal-miners or shop assistants lacked. Because of all this, professionalism's impact on the public domain became increasingly ambiguous. The professional ethic became ever more pervasive, and the public domain ever more extensive, but charges that the ethic had been violated were heard ever more frequently, and there were growing demands for more transparency and accountability.

The Revenge of the Private

Meanwhile, a more subtle threat to the values of the public domain had emerged from a different quarter. I shall call it 'the revenge of the private'. In essence it was a cry of protest against the hard, demanding, 'unnatural' austerities of public duty and public engagement in the name of authenticity and sincerity. In a classic study, Richard Sennett argued that its origins could be traced back to the late nineteenth century;[8]

but its impact on Britain's public culture dates from the 1960s. It conveyed a simple, yet deadly message. The public and private domains ought not to be separate after all: it was, in some profound sense, corrupt, hypocritical and inauthentic to try to separate them; the private self should be omni-competent and omnipresent. In this perspective, the very idea of role-playing – and the public domain is, by definition, a place where public roles are played – was *ipso facto* suspect. The notion that citizenship involves mastering a distinct and difficult set of roles, that the public domain is more like a carefully cultivated garden than an untamed meadow of emotional self-expression, was suspect too. The cry was epitomized in the fashionable feminist slogan, 'The personal is the political'. The slogan contained a germ of truth. The growth of the welfare state, which became a highly charged political issue in the late 1960s and 1970s, was due, in part, to changing patterns of family life – above all, to the growth of female employment outside the home. In an earlier era, opponents of women's suffrage based their case on the per-sonal attributes of the 'weaker sex'. But all too often those who used the slogan forgot another truth: that if the personal is politicized, or the political personalized, the public and private domains are both likely to be twisted out of shape.

The second truth was increasingly forgotten. The period since the Second World War (particularly perhaps in the United States) saw a strange inversion of the Freudian view of the relationship between civilization and the individual psyche. For Freud, repression, and hence neurosis, is the price we pay for civility. His was an essentially tragic view of man as a social animal. We have to repress our instinctual drives for civilization to flourish. We pay a heavy price for doing so; but the alternative is reversion to a Hobbesian state of nature. In the second half of the twentieth century, that Freudian doctrine was stood on its head. An emotionally repressive society, it came to be thought, was a sick society. If the price of civility was repression, then the price was too high. If the values of the public domain necessarily involved emotional distance, a certain coldness, a certain hardness, a certain lack of personal authenticity, then they were emotionally crippling and morally degrading, and therefore deserved to be jettisoned.

A vivid recent example is the cult of Princess Diana, and the flood of public criticism which descended after her death on the older members of the royal family (and, of course, on Prince Charles), on the grounds that their response to their loss showed that they were unfeeling and oppressive. Princess Diana had become an icon for an extraordinarily wide range of commentators, because she had become a symbol of authenticity, of empathy and of suffering. The fact that she was an exceptionally privileged young woman, adept at the arts of self-promotion, was irrelevant. When she died, the royals behaved as they had been taught to do: as symbols of the state, quintessential inhabitants of the public domain, with all its emotional austerity and self-control. But the populace did not want a display of emotional austerity and self-control. They demanded a public display of private grief. In effect, they insisted that the emotions appropriate to the private domain should be put on public display. They wanted bleeding hearts, not just in private but in public too, and they insisted that it was their right to see the blood and judge its quality. Many warned that if the right private emotions were not displayed publicly, then the public role of the royal family would be called into question. For the veteran constitutional reformer, Anthony Barnett, the meaning of Diana's funeral was that

> more people than ever before at a single moment in Britain's history interpreted the meaning of the nation through its relationship to the royals. And the Queen was very definitely not the one who was doing the interpreting. On the contrary, the nation was saying that she was no longer the mirror in which we see our country reflected. We are no longer stiff and buttoned-up; we grieve openly, hug each other and believe in talking through our troubles. . . .

... In a strange way, Britain's first secular Head of State
was installed on 6 September: a President of Hearts.[9]

There were, in short, to be no more barriers between the
private and the public. The same patterns of behaviour were
to prevail in both.

The consequences go wide. One is the rise of an inherently
destructive kind of identity politics. In the eyes of those who
assert them, at any rate, identities are by definition spontaneous and authentic. By virtue of that, they are also non-
negotiable. So are the rituals that embody and fortify them
and the claims that reflect them. Far-right Ulster Protestants,
Jewish settlers in Gaza and on the West Bank, Christian
fundamentalists in the American Bible Belt, Basque supporters
of ETA, and Islamic militants all over the Muslim world
all base their claims to territory or power on their possession of an authentic identity which cannot be compromised
without humiliation. The fact that the identities concerned
are often ersatz, consciously fabricated, rather than uncon-
sciously inherited, does not detract from the claimants'
self-righteousness or indignation. Consider, for example, the
conflicts between Jews and Blacks in parts of New York
City. The Jews boast an authentic and impermeable identity.
So do the Blacks. There can be no compromise between
two rival authenticities; authenticity belongs to the private
domain of feeling, not to the public domain of argument,
debate, reflection and negotiation. Negotiation is pointless if
compromise is impossible; and to compromise one's identity
is to compromise oneself. Once identity is thrown into the
scales, democratic politics – indeed, deliberative politics of
any sort – becomes virtually impossible.

Outside Northern Ireland, Britain's identity politics have,
until recently, had more to do with class than ethnicity. But
class identities can generate as much resentment and bitter-
ness as ethnic ones, as the career of Arthur Scargill, the miners'
leader, shows. In the late 1970s and early 1980s a clamant
proletarianism (often professed by politicians of impeccably

bourgeois origin) played a devastating role in the internal conflicts that helped to keep the Labour Party out of power for eighteen years. The Hon. Anthony Wedgwood Benn, the heir to a peerage who had been educated at Westminster School, was transmogrified into Tony Benn. Not the least of the reasons why James Callaghan became leader of the Labour Party was that, as the political commentator Peter Jenkins put it, he had become the 'Keeper of the Cloth Cap'.[10] These were straws in a dangerous wind. As the old, blue-collar industrial working class shrank in size, its self-styled champions in the Labour Party and the trade unions all too often turned in on themselves in sour and self-destructive resentment. Labour, they convinced themselves, could win power without the progressive intelligentsia which had been an indispensable element in the 'Labour Alliance' since the First World War, and even without the middle-class voters who had helped to give the party its majorities in 1945 and 1966. Truckling to the bourgeoisie was unnecessary, as well as contemptible. What was needed was an uncompromising appeal to working people, designed to radicalize the masses. If this produced a Government of the far right, so much the better: the masses would be radicalized more quickly. The result was the catastrophe of the 1983 election, in which Labour's share of the vote fell to its lowest level since 1918. And class resentment was not confined to the Labour Party. Mrs Thatcher's loathing for the trade unions and, on a deeper level, for the very idea of collective action, was both a symptom of and a vehicle for the insecurities and resentments of the *petit bourgeois* milieu in which she grew up.

The Privatization of Leadership

A further consequence is the privatization of political leadership. For one of the central features of politics in our time is a strange return to the privatism of the pre-modern period. In the eighteenth century, as I tried to show in the last chapter, the distinction between the monarch as a private person and the monarch as the embodiment of public power was still very hazy. In the sixteenth century it did not exist. Henry VIII's marital adventures had direct and, as it turned out, lasting consequences for the English state and church, because monarch and man were the same. In our time, the same is beginning to be true of the elective monarch, whether President or Prime Minister, who heads the state machine. Increasingly we demand of our rulers not just that they be competent at ruling, but that they be authentic human beings as well: that they appear before us unmasked, without disguises, in all their vulnerable humanity. Indeed, we pay more attention to their private selves – or, rather, to what they eagerly display to us as their private selves – than to their public conduct. As Sennett puts it,

> In modern politics it would be suicidal for a leader to insist: Forget about my private life; all you need to know about me is how good a legislator or executive I am and what action I intend to take in office. Instead, we get excited when a conservative French President has dinner with a working-class family, even though he has raised taxes on industrial wages a few days before, or believe an American President is more 'genuine' and reliable than his disgraced predecessor because the new man cooks his own breakfast.[11]

Leadership on these terms, Sennett adds, is a 'form of seduction'.[12]

The seducers pay a heavy price. With extraordinary perversity, we also demand that the private behaviour of our leaders should conform to public norms: that the unmasked, authentic ruler should, in private, live up to exemplary standards which other private persons are not expected to observe. The dangers of this blurring of the private and the public were demonstrated with breath-taking vividness in the extraordinary mixture of farce, hysteria and religiosity that followed the revelation of Bill Clinton's affair with Monica

Lewinsky. Clinton's sexual proclivities became a public issue in a way that would have been unthinkable forty or fifty years ago. (Had it been thinkable, Lloyd George would never have been Prime Minister of Britain, and John F. Kennedy would never have been President of the United States. Even Gladstone, with his bouts of self-flagellation and his penchant for prostitute saving, might have been vulnerable.) And the Clinton–Lewinsky affair is only the most dramatic example of a political genre which has become almost commonplace, at least in the English-speaking world.

The privatization of leadership has gone hand in hand with a set of far-reaching changes in the role and conduct of the media, and in particular of the press. Like barristers, journalists and broadcasters straddle the boundary between the public and market domains. Newspapers and privately owned television channels are market traders. They are subject to intense competitive pressures, for sales and advertising revenue. They can and do go bankrupt. They can also become immensely profitable. But nearly all of them also belong to the public domain. Most newspapers are, in one way or another, political actors in their own right. They have political goals and intervene directly in political debate. Though television channels don't, it is largely through them that the political class communicates with the public. Above all, news and current affairs broadcasts and the news and comment pages of the print media shape public perceptions of political issues and political leaders. This dualism – one foot in the market-place and one foot in the public domain – goes back a long way. In modern times, at least, the media have always had to have one eye on the market-place, but until recently they also played an educational, even civic role. The *Daily Mirror*, a rough, tough popular paper with an enormous circulation, employed Richard Crossman, a quintessential Labour intellectual, as a columnist. The Oxford historian A. J. P. Taylor wrote regularly for the Beaverbrook press. Thanks to technological changes and the emergence of global media empires, however, the competitive pressures which the media have always faced have become far more intense than they used to be, leading mass-circulation papers to sacrifice information for entertainment. Meanwhile, print and broadcast journalists themselves have come to see their roles in a new way. The new privatism of the age has affected them as well as their audiences. They are no longer willing to draw a veil over the private lives of public men and women, as their predecessors did in the days of Gladstone and Lloyd George. Instead, they see themselves as a kind of moral inspectorate, with a duty to police the private, as well as the public, lives of the powerful and well known. Since prurient gossip about scandals in high places sells newspapers and raises ratings, market forces ensure that prurient gossip and the fear of prurient gossip become political forces to be reckoned with.

With all this has come a new version of the politics of connection and patronage which the Gladstonian reformers drove out. Increasingly, the Prime Minister's office in Britain (and still more the White House in the United States) resembles an early-modern court. Of course, this has always been true to some degree. Court politics are a feature of political life in all societies at all times; as long as human beings remain human, and individuals compete for place and power, they will be part of the landscape. But court politics have become far more obtrusive in recent years. To some extent under Thatcher, and far more under Blair, the Cabinet has virtually ceased to exist. What counts is access to the monarch's person, just as it did under Henry VIII and Louis XIV. And access is increasingly divorced from public roles. Under Blair, Peter Mandelson, Alastair Campbell, Jonathan Powell, young and unheard-of members of the Policy Unit, Cabinet ministers and long-serving senior civil servants, jostle for the prince's ear, as their forerunners jostled in the courts of early-modern times. Though the process accelerated sharply in the 1980s and 1990s, it was already in evidence before then. In the Wilson governments of the 1960s, the no. 10 'kitchen cabinet' was notorious – more notorious, perhaps, than its influence on policy merited. In the 1970s, court politics were institutionalized by the creation of a Policy Unit of personal appointees to advise the Prime Minister and by the emergence of a network of ministerial 'special advisers', who also owed their posts to the personal favour of their bosses.

Just before the passage of the 1867 Reform Act, Walter Bagehot famously distinguished between the 'dignified' and the 'efficient' elements in the British Constitution. The function of the dignified elements was to bamboozle the masses into accepting the hidden reality of bourgeois power. The real rulers, 'secreted in second-rate carriages', were obeyed because the masses deferred to the pomp and circumstance of the 'apparent rulers' at the head of the social procession. And the monarch was, of course, the most 'dignified' element of all. However, Bagehot's picture of the glittering monarchical show concealing the drab reality of bourgeois power is now out of date. The monarchical show and the reality of power are beginning to coincide once again – not, of course, in the sense that the actual monarch exercises power, but in the sense that the elective monarch increasingly behaves in the way that monarchs behaved in the days before the modern state came into being. Unfortunately, privatist politics devours its children. Where the monarchs of old drew their legitimacy from God, today's elective monarch depends on the shifting sands of popular and media favour; and when the populace and the media withdraw their support, as they invariably do sooner or later, it is not easily rebuilt. It is not an accident that monarchical populism has gone hand in hand with ebbing legitimacy. Against the background of this and the other developments I have sketched in this chapter, I turn, in the next two chapters, to the recent past and the current state of the public domain.

4

Kulturkampf

Despite the tribulations described in the last chapter, the public domain of the early 1970s still seemed invulnerable. Ten years later, it was under siege – the target of a passionate neoliberal crusade which was to transform the political and moral economies in the 1980s and 1990s. The crusade has attracted a vast literature, and only the broad outlines need recalling here. The crusaders operated on two levels – economic and moral or cultural. In economics, they were the children (or perhaps the grandchildren) of the *laissez-faire* utopians excoriated by Karl Polanyi. Their goal was an idealized market, free of distortions, working in the way that the axioms of classical political economy said markets worked. In their eyes, the Keynesian revolution was intellectually nonsensical and practically disastrous. The notion that the level of employment could be determined by the central state was absurd. Unemployment occurred when workers forced real wages above the market-clearing price for labour. Mopping it up by demand management merely debauched the currency, creating further unemployment in the long run. Despite its doctrinal purity and long lineage, however, the tradition of economic liberalism to which the crusaders adhered was confined to a small minority for a quarter of a century after the Second World

War. Its adherents were fanatically convinced of their own rationality and rectitude, but theirs was the fanaticism of the outsider, with more than a hint of resentment about it. They saw themselves as prophets crying in the wilderness, spurning the flesh-pots of a sloppy, pusillanimous Establishment to preach an unpopular truth.

It was not until the mid-1970s that neo-liberal political economy came in from the cold. It did so because accelerating economic decline, industrial unrest, a plummeting pound, soaring inflation and, above all, a perceived threat of ungovernability gave the neo-liberal critique of the mixed economy and the extended state new weight, and the neo-liberal alternative, new plausibility. The policy and institutional paradigm of the post-war period – broadly Keynesian economic management carried out by a state machine imbued with the tradition of autonomous executive power – was manifestly bankrupt. Whatever their ideological preferences, decision-makers were forced to look for new approaches. The political left offered only more of the same, dressed up in rebarbative *Marxisant* rhetoric. The neo-liberals offered a clean break with the recent past – balanced budgets, strict control of the money supply, price stability, market solutions in place of producer-group appeasement. It was no contest. Well before electoral battle was joined, the neo-liberals had won the battle of ideas.

In their own eyes, the moral or cultural dimension of their crusade was more important than the economic. It was epitomized in Margaret Thatcher's evocation of her Grantham upbringing. For her, she wrote in her memoirs, the first lesson to be drawn from the war 'was that the kind of life that the people of Grantham had lived before the war was a decent and wholesome one'. In a later passage she added, 'My "Bloomsbury" was Grantham – Methodism, the grocer's shop, Rotary and all the serious sober virtues cultivated and esteemed in that environment.'[1] As she saw it, the purpose of the neo liberal revolution of the 1980s was not primarily economic. It was to revive the 'serious, sober virtues' of her

Grantham past. As she put it herself, 'economics are the method, the object is to change the heart and soul'.[2] Market forces were better than state intervention, not just because they were more efficient, but because the market-place was quintessentially the realm of freedom, and because only free people can be moral agents. Thrift, enterprise and self-reliance were, of course, the building blocks of a prosperous economy. But that was not the chief reason for valuing them. They were also the stigmata of the 'vigorous virtues' – virtues whose possessors were, as Shirley Letwin put it, 'upright, self-sufficient, energetic, adventurous, independent-minded, loyal to friends and robust against enemies'.[3]

Hayek struck essentially the same chord in the third volume of his great book *Law, Legislation and Liberty*. A market order could flourish only if the values appropriate to it prevailed, he pointed out. These

> were inevitably learned by all the members of a population consisting chiefly of independent farmers, artisans and apprentices. . . . They held an ethos that esteemed the prudent man, the good husbandman and provider who looked after the future of his family and his business by building up capital, guided less by the desire to consume much than by the wish to be regarded as successful by his fellows. . . .
>
> At present, however, an ever-increasing part of the population of the Western world grow up . . . as strangers to those rules of the market which have made the great society possible. To them, the market economy is largely incomprehensible; they have never practised the rules on which it rests and its results seem to them irrational and immoral.[4]

For Hayek the growth of collectivism was to be deplored – above all, because it had eroded the prudent market ethos of the past. By the same token, Mrs Thatcher condemned the 'dependency culture' created by the collectivist interventionism of the preceding century or so, not just because it ate into the public purse, but because it turned those it entrapped into 'moral cripples'. 'Victorian values' were extolled, not just because they had prevailed in the days of Britain's glory, but also because they were morally right. Collective action and collective provision were not only sources of inflationary overload. Much more damagingly, they were sources of moral escapism, enabling those who took part in them to shelter from the consequences of their own actions, and engendering a corrosive culture of guilt, pervaded by 'a familiar rhetoric: caring, compassion and consensus, the three fudging Cs'.[5] In the neo-liberal crusade, these two elements, the economic and the moral, were fused. Some crusaders gave more emphasis to the first, others to the second. But almost all of them believed that they were fighting for clear-sighted economic rationality against confusion, muddle and wishful thinking, and, at the same time, for stern and enduring moral verities against decadent self-indulgence. The righteous fervour that gave them their *élan* was rooted in this fusion.

Both elements were intrinsically hostile to the public domain. Neo-liberal economics challenged the central premiss on which its champions had based their case. At the heart of the neo-liberal economic vision lay the notion of the rational, self-interested individual utility maximizer. But for the champions of the public domain, individuals are not only, or in all circumstances, self-interested utility maximizers. They can and do transcend individual utility maximization for the sake of the public interest; they are motivated, at least in part, and for some of the time, by a sense of service and of civic duty. Individual utility maximization reigns only in the market domain; in the public domain it does not. For the neo-liberals, a public domain so defined was an impossibility, as was the notion of a public interest which was more than the sum of private interests. The proposition that it was possible to transcend individual utility maximization – except, of course, in the private domain – was absurd. Those who claimed to do so were camouflaging self-interest in an inherently deceitful rhetoric of civic virtue. When Mrs Thatcher famously said that there was no such thing as society, but only individuals and their families, she epitomized this aspect of the neo-liberal creed.

In the moral or cultural sphere, matters were more complicated. When Shirley Letwin celebrated the 'vigorous virtues',
or Margaret Thatcher the 'serious, sober virtues', they implied
that market rationality was not enough: that rational economic agents ought to abide by a supra-rational moral code
of some sort. But New Right virtues and the civic virtues of
the public domain belonged to different moral universes. For
the New Right, virtue went with independence, and independence with self-reliance. The pre-collectivist Hayekian
individual was a moral being because he stood on his own
feet and made his own choices. But, as I argued in chapter 2,
the champions of the public domain posited an *interdependent*
society, in which those who stood successfully on their own
feet and those who did not were partners in a common
venture. For the neo-liberals, such talk was humbug – a manifestation of middle-class guilt, an excuse for fecklessness
and self-indulgence. True morality was private, not public;
individual, not social. Virtuous individuals did good works,
but they did them out of the goodness of their private hearts.
They were not – and by definition could not be – bound to
the beneficiaries by ties of mutual obligation. The very
language of the public domain – a 'public' conscience, 'civic'
virtue, the 'collectivization' of risk – was implicitly immoral.
The mentality behind it had to be rooted out.

Why the Neo-liberals Won

All this helps to explain the ideological passion which char-
acterized the neo-liberal crusade of the 1970s and 1980s; but
it does not explain why the crusaders should have dominated
the political stage for nearly twenty years, or why their legacy
should still be ubiquitous. Six reasons stand out. In the first
place, neo-liberal political economy ran with the grain of the
resurgent privatism of the age. The neo-liberals wished to
put Exit in place of Voice: market relationships in place of
political ones. Now Exit is, almost by definition, expressive,

free and spontaneous. It is individualistic and, in a profound sense, private. The ties of loyalty are set aside, because they have come to seem oppressive, unsatisfying or self-stultifying to the *individual*. Central to the privatist renaissance were the values of authenticity, of direct experience, of all that was implied in the fashionable solipsism, 'doing your own thing'. Emotionally, perhaps even intellectually, those values are first cousins to the values of market liberalism. The freely choosing consumer, making her own decisions, standing on her own feet and spending her own money in her own way, without having to pay heed to externally imposed constraints, is first cousin to the authentic individual celebrated by the new privatism. Who could be more authentic than a shopper roaming the aisles of Sainsbury's in search of the brand of yoghurt that expresses her individuality best?

The second reason for the neo-liberals' success is that they offered a seductively simple answer to the lack of accountability which had done so much to undermine the authority of the extended state and to force professionals on to the defensive. The bamboozled, frustrated citizen and the patronized client would be reborn as empowered, liberated customers. The crystalline simplicities of contract would replace the tortuous negotiations of politics, and cut through the self-serving pieties of the professional ethic. Condescending bureaucrats and haughty professionals would be exposed to competitive pressures, simulating those of the market-place or emanating directly from it. Like Schumpeter, and for essentially the same reasons as Schumpeter, neo-liberals held that the classic model of active citizenship, which the champions of the public domain had invoked so powerfully in the nineteenth century, was based on self-deception. It could not work in a complex modern society. But that was only the beginning. At the same time, said the neo-liberals, the realistic, hard-nosed, Schumpeterian model of democratic citizenship, in which the task of the citizen was merely to choose between rival teams of political leaders, led inevitably to overload, inflation and the associated evils that came to a head in the 1970s.

The conclusion was stark: neither the participatory nor the Schumpeterian model of political accountability was compatible with free-market capitalism. The participatory model was incompatible because it presupposed a politics for which large-scale modern societies had no place. The Schumpeterian model was not open to that objection. The form of accountability it offered – essentially, 'Kick the rascals out' – was perfectly feasible. The trouble was that this kind of accountability fostered a supermarket conception of politics, with political leaders as policy salesmen and voters as customers, that undermined the capitalist free market by engendering inflation and overload. All this led to the simple conclusion that the only way to ensure accountability without endangering capitalism was drastically to cut down the public realm and, wherever possible, to substitute accountability through markets or proxy markets (and to some extent through law) for accountability through politics. And what applied to the relationship between providers and users of public policy also applied to the relationship between providers and users of professional services. Central to the notion of the professional ethic was the assertion that professionals could be trusted because they were professionals, because they had been socialized into their own particular version of the civic ideal. That was as resounding a nonsense, said the neo-liberals, as the parallel assertion that twentieth-century political leaders could realize an ideal ultimately derived from the city-states of ancient Greece and Rome. Here, as elsewhere, the only feasible key to accountability was marketization.

Thirdly, neo-liberalism offered a ready-made explanation for the repeated policy failures of the 1960s and 1970s. At the heart of the case for the mixed economy lay the notion of market failure. State intervention was needed because markets failed. The great rhetorical achievement of the neo-liberals was to turn that argument on its head. Governments also failed, they pointed out: and Government failure was unavoidable. No Government could possibly know enough to second-guess the unpredictable transactions of dispersed market actors. In any case, governments were not composed of disinterested Platonic guardians, solely concerned to promote the public good, as the advocates of the mixed economy implicitly presupposed. Politicians were market traders too, but of a very special kind. They were subject to the imperatives of the Vote market, blown hither and thither by the gusts of electoral expediency. The bureaucracies over which they presided were not disinterested either. Bureaucrats had axes to grind, careers to make, and empires to build. The extended state, which had come into being to correct the supposed failures of the market, was less a cure than a disease. Far from extending it – as governments of both parties had done for most of the post-war period – the task was to prune it back. This was a more paradoxical conclusion than it seemed at first sight. The neo-liberals were proposing a politics of anti-politics; and on their own assumptions such a politics was impossible. But it was an attractive paradox at a time when the old political approaches led nowhere.

The fourth reason goes wider. The promise of an anti-political politics was given extra bite by an elite of anti-elitists. Nothing had done more to discredit the state or to undermine the public domain than the decomposition of the elites which had managed them. In the 1960s and 1970s, the stable, essentially late Victorian structure of authority and consent, which the political and professional classes had still taken for granted in the early post-war period, collapsed. But no new structure took its place. Only the corporate elite that dominated the market domain could emulate the authority and self-confidence which had once marked the elites of the public domain. By a convenient paradox, this corporate elite appealed to two contradictory emotions at the same time. It was, by any reckoning, an elite. It consisted of successful, powerful, well-rewarded people, basking in the authority of success and supported by complex hierarchies. But, in its own eyes at any rate, it was also an anti-elite, and it was surprisingly successful in presenting itself as such. Corporate leaders depicted themselves as heroes out of Samuel Smiles, who had risen by their own efforts in the hard world of wealth creation. Whereas Whitehall mandarins, health-service consultants and university professors merely climbed settled career ladders, corporate leaders rose by 'adding value' through competitive struggle. The corporate elite was not particularly neo-liberal in behaviour; the rigours of genuinely free competition, of the sort extolled in neo-liberal doctrine, have never had much attraction for business leaders. But it had become increasingly suspicious of the public domain as a source of resource wastage, excessive taxation and inflation, and on the principle of 'my enemy's enemy is my friend' it leaped aboard the neo-liberal bandwagon and gave it a further push.

The fifth reason went wider still. The travails of the British economy in the 1970s were not exclusively British in origin. They were due, at least in part, to a transformation of the global political economy which was beginning to make itself felt in the late 1960s, and which still continues at the start of the twenty-first century. The currently fashionable name for this transformation is 'globalization'; in the 1970s and 1980s it was more common to speak of 'interdependence'. But the name does not matter. What matters is that the third quarter of the twentieth century saw a world-wide capitalist renaissance fostered by (and in turn fostering) the emergence of a global market-place for goods, services and, above all, capital, which the Keynesian policy paradigm of the post-war period could not encompass. To summarize crudely, Keynesianism in one country became economically unfeasible. Global Keynesianism was politically unfeasible, since there was no global government to put it into practice. As a result, the neo-liberal paradigm triumphed almost everywhere. British neo-liberals were more doctrinaire and more messianic than most of their counterparts elsewhere, but they swam with a global current. That said, it is important to note that Britain was not *obliged* to take part in the capitalist renaissance in the way that she did. There is more than one model of capitalism, and in principle British governments could have opted for a different one. Though there was a lively debate about possible alternatives in the academic community, however, it made virtually no impact on the political class. As a result, the neo-liberals could plausibly claim that they and they alone could address economic realities that now circled the globe.

Finally, the neo-liberals appeared able to solve the problems of governability, social control and civic discipline which had loomed increasingly large in the strife-torn 1970s. Fears of ungovernability, indiscipline and a breakdown of social control were not new. They had figured repeatedly in the debates over the extension of the suffrage in the nineteenth century. In the twentieth century, such fears subsided, in large part thanks to the experience of the two world wars. The masses, it turned out, were as willing to sacrifice themselves for their country as the classes. By the 1970s, however, wartime memories had faded. The rhetoric of collective self-discipline had lost its purchase. The spectre of a Hobbesian war of all against all, fuelled by brute sectional self-interest, increasingly haunted the imagination of the political class. Against that background, the neo-liberal critique of the ethic and institutions of the public domain was hard to answer. Civic virtue, they declared, was and always had been a broken reed. For the civically virtuous were bound to be exploited by unvirtuous free-riders. Public trust was therefore bound to be betrayed. The inevitable result was a *sauve qui peut* – a race for the bottom, impelled by the growing weight of mistrust. Yet social discipline had to be restored somehow or other. The solution was to turn to the disciplines of the market-place, or, when they were not available, to those of proxy markets. For the custodians of the public domain, this was an unpalatable argument. Yet, as time went on, many of them were at least half-persuaded by it.

The Paradox of Neo-liberalism

Market disciplines would not spring to life in an economy weighed down by a bloated state. State contraction was therefore fundamental to the neo-liberal project. By a paradox reminiscent of post-revolutionary Russia, however, the road to a slimmed-down state ran through state aggrandizement. The most important instrument for slimming it down was privatization; and privatization usually implied regulation. Most of the candidates for it were natural monopolies. (That was why they had been nationalized in the first place.) If they were left unregulated after they had been sold off, consumers would have no protection against their monopoly power. In much of the public sector, moreover, privatization was politically unfeasible. (The National Health Service is the prime example.) There marketization had to be a substitute for privatization: proxy markets, audits, assessments and similar devices had to do the job which market competition could not do. Obvious questions arose. Who were the regulators to be? By whom were they to be appointed? Who would lay down the rules which they would have to follow? Who would oversee the proxy markets, design the audits, and make sure that they achieved their purposes? The only possible answer was that these things would have to be done by public officials, appointed in the last resort by Government, and operating in a way determined by Government. In short, the neo-liberal state was still a state. It turned out to be at least as interventionist as the old mixed-economy state. In some ways, it was more so: the regulators bore down on the privatized companies more heavily than ministers had borne down on their nationalized predecessors. A purist neo-liberal could be forgiven for thinking that privatization did little more than rearrange the deck-chairs on the *Titanic*.

On a deeper level, Hayek's nostalgia for the values of a pre-collectivist age turned out to be double-edged. He was right that these values had been eroded by the social and cultural changes of the preceding 100 years. But in that case, only radical cultural surgery could resurrect the liberal economy for which he and his fellow neo-liberals yearned. There could be no cultural surgery without a cultural surgeon – a paradoxical notion for a Hayekian. The values of the public domain had become so deeply entrenched in the century between Gladstone's first Government and the crises of the 1970s that a mere change of policy at the centre could not eradicate them. They were embodied in, and transmitted by, a host of institutions, practices, implicit assumptions and instinctive reflexes. It was utopian to expect them to fade away merely because ministers had abandoned Keynesian economics or sold off public assets. The institutions had to be forced into a different mould. The practices had to change – or be changed. The implicit assumptions had to be turned inside out. The reflexes had to be unlearned. New economic policies, designed to revive the free market, would not be enough. As long as the collectivist mentality of the last sixty years survived, such policies would be frustrated. That mentality had to be swept away, and only a strong, intrusive and aggressive state could do this.

That was only the beginning. Not only was state power needed to free the economy from the encumbrances created by a century of collectivism; it was needed just as much to keep the economy free, once the first stage of the neo-liberal project had been accomplished. For neo-liberalism offered its votaries no resting-place; no end-point, after which struggle would cease. The threat of backsliding could never be banished: 'socialism', Thatcher memorably declared, 'is never defeated'.[6] Without a strong state to keep on watering it, the soil in which the vigorous virtues had been so laboriously replanted would dry up. A dependency culture would creep back; distortions would once again impede the free play of market forces. For there is, of course, a paradox about market relationships. Left to themselves, freely choosing market actors are notoriously prone to choose collusion in preference to competition; given half a chance, they will band together to win monopoly rents for themselves at the expense of society at large. Only a strong, determined state, run by consistent market liberals, could stop them. In practice, moreover, the *laissez-faire* utopia of the market liberals of the 1980s, like the *laissez-faire* utopia of the early nineteenth century, was inherently unfeasible. Since it presupposed a conception of the human self which ran counter to psychological – and perhaps even to biological – realities, it could never come fully into existence. Like a mirage gleaming in the desert, it drew its pursuers deeper and deeper into the sands. But the pursuers could not allow themselves to recognize the mirage for what it was. They had to press on. Like the Stalinists in post-revolutionary Russia or the Maoists during the Cultural Revolution, they had to find new enemies to vanquish, new traitors to punish, new evils to uproot. In practice, only a powerful state could do the vanquishing, punishing and uprooting. The dawn of Hayekian freedom in a limited state would have to wait.

A crucial question followed. Where would the neo-liberal state find the strength it needed? For many neo-liberals, the preferred answer was tradition: the Constitution of the Founding Fathers in the United States; the absolutely sovereign Crown in Parliament in Britain. Unfortunately, that answer led nowhere. In Britain, at any rate, the state tradition was broken-backed. The Victorian Constitution had vanished for ever. The Constitution of the mid-twentieth century – the Constitution lauded by Leo Amory – had lost, or was rapidly losing, legitimacy. Given all this, only one answer was left. The neo-liberal state would have to derive its strength from the direct, unmediated popular will. The people, neo-liberals told themselves, were sound at heart. Once liberated from corrupting vested interests, they would respond appropriately to the neo-liberal message. And so neo-liberal politics became populist as well as anti-political.

The Magic of Populism

The implications were far-reaching. Populism is not a doctrine. It is a disposition, an approach, a *style*. For populists, wisdom and virtue, an intuitive unschooled wisdom all the more profound for being unschooled, and an instinctive, innocent virtue uncorrupted by excessive ratiocination, reside in the people, and not in any elite or institution. 'Romania?' said an anonymous Romanian philosopher at an international philosophy conference some time ago, 'My country's contribution to philosophy is the immemorial wisdom of the Rumanian peasant.'[7] That is the populist vision in a nutshell. Peasants are wiser than philosophers: the people are right, and the Establishment is wrong. Values are not in tension with each other, and there is no need for the negotiation and debate which were fundamental to the civic ideal. The people decide which values are to prevail. In extreme versions of the populist approach, they even decide what is scientifically valid – as when that archetypal American populist, William Jennings Bryan, insisted that evolution should not be taught in the public school system because 'not one in ten of those who accept the bible as the word of God' believed it to be true.

By the same token, legitimate power springs from the uncorrupted people, and only from the people. Constitutional checks and balances are therefore suspect. They impede the expressions of the popular will, and chop up the power which emanates from the people into self-stultifying bits. Besides, there is no need for them. The people are a homogeneous and monolithic whole. There is no need to protect minorities from the tyranny of the majority. Minorities are either part of the whole, in which case they need no protection, or self-excluded from it, in which case they do not deserve to be protected. Apparent differences of interest or value that cut across the body of the people, that divide the collective sovereign against itself, are products of elite manipulation or, in Margaret Thatcher's immortal phrase, of 'the enemy within'. For there is a strong paranoid streak in the populist mentality. Against the pure, virtuous people stand corrupt, privileged elites and sinister, conspiratorial subversives. The latter are for ever plotting to do down the former.

The implications for political leadership are particularly striking. Populist leaders appeal to the emotions I have tried

to describe, and claim to share them. But there is a large
element of humbug in this. Even leaders who originally sprang
from the ranks of the people no longer belong to the ranks,
once they start to lead. Populist leaders have to come to
terms with this awkward fact. Characteristically, they do so
by laying claims to a special, intuitive, supra-rational understanding of the people and of their values and beliefs. Charles
de Gaulle, Enoch Powell, Adolph Hitler, David Lloyd George
did not need to find out what the people thought. They knew.
They knew because their hearts beat in time with the
people's. Sometimes the results have been ludicrous, as when
Tony Benn demanded and got a referendum on European
Community membership, only to see his side of the argument
crushingly defeated. Sometimes they have been evil, as with
Hitler. Sometimes they have been magnificent, as with de
Gaulle. What matters, however, is the psychic mechanism
through which the results are achieved. Populist leaders
believe that they embody the popular will, that they have a
private line to that will, that they can and should appeal to it
directly without going through intermediaries. Buoyed up by
that belief, they offer certainty, security and glamour in place
of the drab, confusing greys of the ordinary politician. While
the magic lasts, the rewards are great. The German socialist
Egon Wertheimer once described Ramsay MacDonald, in his
day a heroic figure, as 'the focus for the mute hopes of a
class'.[8] Substitute 'people' for 'class', and that is the essence
of populist leadership.

   In the case of Margaret Thatcher, the Coeur de Lion of
Britain's neo-liberal crusade, the magic lasted for a remarkably long time. In a sense untrue of any previous peacetime
Prime Minister, with the possible exception of Lloyd George,
her style was both populist and charismatic. She was, of
course, leader of the Conservative Party and head of the
Government; as such, she controlled a formidable battery of
institutional power. But in her own eyes, at least, her authority came direct from the people, not from the institutions
over which she presided. In reality, of course, she did not

embody the popular will; there is no such thing. Like most populist leaders, she constructed it. But that only made her claim to embody it more insistent. When institutions are in disarray, when the elites that ran them have been discredited, when an old order has fallen apart, and there is no coherent alternative in sight, the easiest way to legitimize public policy is to turn to the sovereign people. That was Thatcher's great discovery, and she put it into practice with consummate skill. Again and again, she appealed to the voters over the heads of the battered intermediate institutions of yesteryear. Her reward was a new social coalition, buttressed by, and in turn buttressing, a form of governance with no recent precedent. The ponderous, cumbersome, but at the same time thorough and systematic processes of consultation and discussion which had previously preceded important policy innovations – the Royal Commissions, civil service cogitations and interest-group representations – were bypassed or swept aside. Whitehall became a machine for turning neo-liberal intimations into policy, as rapidly as possible. The ideal public servant ceased to be a non-partisan policy adviser, and became a superior mechanic.

It hardly needs saying that this approach struck hard at the foundations of the public domain. Populism is monist. Populists seek to concentrate the popular will so that it flows into a single channel. The logic of the public domain is quintessentially pluralist. It grew up higgledy-piggledy, in response to particular pressures. Variety is of its essence. Though Britain has never had a fundamental law entrenching the checks and balances on which pluralist politics depend, informal codes, inherited usages and unwritten rules nurtured a vast range of more or less autonomous intermediate institutions, public and private. These codes, usages and rules were the perimeter walls of the public domain as it grew up in the ninety-odd years after Gladstone's *Nineteenth Century* article. The civic ideal that fuelled its growth and still lingers in the memories of its defenders stresses debate, engagement and participation – values alien to the populist vision of a single, undifferentiated people. In the civic ideal, the wider society is a mosaic of smaller collectivities, with differing interests and purposes. Leadership is essential to popular government, but leaders do not – indeed, cannot – embody the popular will. The people are not a homogeneous lump. In any case, they can be wrong as well as right. The roar of popular approval is no guarantee of political wisdom. Democratic self-government depends on tolerance, on a willingness to listen to others, on the capacity to distinguish between private interests and the public interest. These qualities do not come naturally. They have to be learned; and they are learned in the intermediate institutions that populists instinctively abhor.

The Logic of Hegemony

The combination of populism and neo-liberalism made a heady brew. The neo-liberal crusade started modestly, but its ambitions grew with success. By the mid-1980s, its leaders had embarked on a self-conscious, highly sophisticated and astonishingly radical programme of cultural reconstruction, more far-reaching than anything attempted by any British Government since the days of Oliver Cromwell, and more reminiscent of Gramscian Marxism than of anything in the British conservative tradition. Their aim was to replace the 'dependency culture' of the collectivist past with an 'enterprise culture', modelled on the United States and Victorian Britain. For David Young, corporate grandee turned neo-liberal politician, the essence of the enterprise culture lay in 'the restoration of the age of the individual'.[9] For Nigel Lawson, who claimed to have coined the term, it meant that

> we were seeking not simply to remove various controls and impositions, but by doing so *to change the entire culture of a nation* from anti-profits, anti-business, government-dependent

104

lassitude and defeatism, to a pro-profit, pro-business, robustly independent vigour and optimism . . . based on self-belief and the will to succeed. Defeatism, the characteristic of pre-Thatcher Britain, is invariably self-fulfilling.[10]

These formulations bristled with paradox. The whole edifice of neo-liberal economics rests on the assumption that individuals are the best judges of their own interests. Young, Lawson and their ministerial colleagues stood that assumption on its head. They wished to engineer a cultural revolution from the top down. The only possible justification for such a project was that they knew better than the society they had been elected to govern what its true interests were. But in neo-liberal eyes, that was not a paradox at all. If the freely choosing individual of neo-liberal doctrine made choices that conflicted with the axioms of economic liberalism, that only proved that there were even more obstacles to the free flow of market forces than they had imagined, and that the neo-liberal state had to try, even more energetically, to overcome them. Undeterred by charges of incoherence, the cultural revolution drove on.

The result was a long-drawn-out, bitterly fought *kulturkampf* between that state and the ethic, culture and operational codes of the public domain. The neo-liberals were trying to reverse Polanyi's counter-movement against early-nineteenth-century *laissez-faire* utopianism; to extirpate the legacy of the long cultural revolution which had made the growth of the public domain possible in the first place. They sought to change behaviour by changing beliefs, and to change beliefs by changing behaviour. To succeed, they had to demolish the ideological and institutional barriers that protected the public domain from incursions by the market domain. They had to root out anti-market (and even non-market) values and assumptions, and make sure that they did not reappear. They also had to re-engineer public discourse: to silence or at least to marginalize the language in which such values and assumptions were expressed, and by which they were fortified. They had to capture or neutralize the institutions that embodied and transmitted them, and discredit the practices that stemmed from them. Above all, they had to entrench their changes in the political culture. Their crusade did not follow a predetermined path, derived from a carefully considered strategy. Contingency and improvisation loomed as large as they usually do in political life. All the same, an inner logic ran through the whole project: the logic of hegemony.

The Grovel Count

The most obvious barrier to a neo-liberal hegemony was the state-owned industrial sector. Between 1979 and 1997 almost all nationalized concerns were sold off at bargain prices ('privatized' in the neo-liberal jargon), in most cases to the great financial benefit of their managers. In addition, one and a quarter million council houses were sold to their tenants. On one level, the results were unremarkable. Public attitudes were not transformed; market forces were not freed from the dead hand of the state; the dream of a people's capitalism did not materialize. The privatized public utilities soon became bitterly unpopular. Obtrusive (and often controversial) state-sponsored regulation was a far cry from the invisible hand of the market. The long-term trend to concentrate share ownership in institutional hands continued unabated.[11] Yet for Thatcher herself, privatization was the chief weapon in the neo-liberal armoury; and her verdict deserves to be taken seriously. To the extent that privatization helped to keep public borrowing and taxation low – its real justification in the eyes of most Conservative ministers – it helped her to build the social coalition I referred to earlier. On a deeper level, it signalled the demise of the common sense of the post-war period – that even in a capitalist economy the public interest is sometimes best served by state ownership; that if private owners fail to honour their obligations to the public interest, they can and should be expropriated. It also helped to entrench a new one: that private firms are always more efficient than governments; that private property rights are so sacrosanct that they must be created where they do not already exist; and that the mixed economy is a slippery slope leading to collectivist perdition.

Publicly owned undertakings were a soft target. More formidable barriers to the neo-liberal project had to be tackled as well. Chief among them was the senior civil service: the most important legacy of the nineteenth-century campaign against 'Old Corruption' and the chief guarantor of the integrity of the public domain. Professional, non-partisan, career civil servants served the public by definition. The values by which they lived their professional lives ran counter to those of the market-place, and also to those of the private domain. Their very existence presupposed a public interest transcending private interests, in a sense not true of other civilian professions, with the possible exception of officials in local government. They were not supposed to define the public interest; that was a task for ministers, accountable to Parliament. But they *were* supposed to pursue and defend it – if necessary by acting as a counterweight to the inevitable short-termism of their political masters. For they were the institutional memory – the hard disk – of the state. Ministers decided, but civil servants advised; and their advice distilled not just their own experience, but that of the whole state machine. To do this, they had to be personally disinterested and detached from the party battle. Their advice had to be honest and impartial; they had to tell their masters the truth as they saw it, without fear or favour, and their masters had to know that their advice was untainted by party affiliations. To make all this possible, they had to be recruited on merit, through open competition, and their career paths had to be immune from political intervention. That in turn meant that their presence at the heart of the state was a crucial safeguard, both against a lurch back into the favouritism and nepotism of the eighteenth and early nineteenth centuries and against infiltration by the 'universal pandar' of market power.

This was an ideal. It was not always practised. Some civil servants became the creatures of ministers; some crossed the line between policy advice and policy making; some shrank from the obligation to tell their masters unwelcome truths. To the commissars of the neo-liberal cultural revolution, however, the ideal itself was anathema, not the occasional deviations from it. On neo-liberal assumptions, the career civil service was doubly suspect. Bureaucratic empire building was one of the drivers of government failure; the bureaucrats' non-market values embodied and transmitted the collectivist ethos which had brought the country to its knees. As an incorrigibly elitist intermediate institution, whose task was to take a long view, the civil service was an obstacle to the populist politics from which the revolutionaries drew their strength. To the elites of the market domain (and to many ministers), it was a refuge for wimps and faint hearts who lacked the energy, toughness and flair for wealth creation. To virtually all the revolutionaries, the detachment on which it prided itself was a cloak for defeatism at best, and for obstruction at worst.

Few had the stomach for a switch to an American-style spoils system, ensuring that party supporters of the ministers of the day would hold the top civil service posts. But high-level appointments were frequently filled by business tycoons, ideologically acceptable to ministers; and the governments of the 1980s and 1990s did their best to force the culture of the existing civil service into a new mould, fit for an enterprise culture. Their policies were not all of a piece. Some of the changes they introduced had been advocated in debates on civil service reform in the heyday of the Keynesian era, when neo-liberalism was still confined to the political fringe. Some owed as much to civil servants as to ministers. Some were borrowed from left-of-centre regimes abroad. By the same token, the process of change was too complex for a brief summary to do justice to it. For the purposes of this book, however, what matters is the broad thrust, not the details. And the thrust is clear. In the perspective of the neo-liberal revolution, there was no intrinsic difference between the state and a private firm. Both had customers whom they had to satisfy and resources which they had to deploy as efficiently as possible. Therefore, both had to be managed in essentially the same way.

Some state activities could be off-loaded directly into the market sphere: that was the point of privatization. Some could not. Wherever possible, activities thought to be unsuitable for outright privatization were devolved to so-called agencies. These were supposed to operate at arm's length from ministers, and their managers were supposed to behave as though they were running private firms. (Since the activities in question were often highly political, both objectives turned out to be unachievable in practice.) All this slimmed down the administrative civil service of old days quite drastically, but an irreducible rump remained in the central departments. The rump could not be privatized or marketized, but subtler methods could – and did – transform its mentality. Ministers made it clear that dispassionate advice and careful argument were out. 'Can-do' problem solving (framed, of course, by the assumptions of neo-liberal political economy and the requirements of populist governance) was in. To make sure that problem-solvers prospered, and dispassionate advisers suffered, Thatcher, as Prime Minister, took an unprecedently close interest in promotions to the most senior posts. The introduction of performance-related pay rubbed home the message: Northcote–Trevelyan was no more; civil servants were no longer expected to tell the truth to power. If 'politics' means party politics, charges that the senior civil service was politicized during the Thatcher years were wide of the mark: by no means all the beneficiaries of Thatcher's interventions were Conservative in the party sense. But in a phrase coined by Lord Bancroft, head of the civil service when Mrs Thatcher came to power, the 'grovel count' rose sharply.[12] Those who could not bring themselves to grovel languished or left. Inevitably, those who grovelled slowly internalized the crucial axioms of the Government's ideology and statecraft. The scandal revealed by the Scott Report is eloquent testimony to the results.

The War against Institutions

The disinterested, dispassionate career civil service of old days was not the only candidate for cultural reconstruction. In neo-liberal eyes, a whole gamut of public-service institutions, ranging from the universities to the Church of England and from schools to the National Health Service, was equally in need of it. Even the police were not above suspicion. Not all these institutions were brought to heel: the Church of England was a bone in the Government's throat to the end. However, few escaped the cultural revolution unscathed. Their fates differed in detail, but the differences were trivial compared to the similarities. In virtually every institution, eighteen years of neo-liberalism exalted managers, often recruited from the corporate sector, at the expense of the professionals who formed the backbone of the institution concerned. Everywhere, professional autonomy was curtailed, and wherever possible, the stable career paths protecting it were disrupted. Real markets were not available, but ingenious proxy markets, designed to force professionals into the enterprise culture, further undermined the barriers between the public and the market domains.

At the same time, professional performance was increasingly subjected to audits, mimicking those used to appraise managerial performance in the corporate sector. They differed in detail from profession to profession, but once again the differences mattered less than the similarities. Underlying all of them was the neo-liberal assumption that professions were at bottom self-interested producer cartels, seeking monopoly rents. It followed that they could not be trusted to appraise themselves, and that the cosy systems of self-regulation which had once been part and parcel of professional life had to be replaced (or at least supplemented) by disinterested, transparent, external audit. There was, of course, a paradox here. The auditors were themselves professionals; unless they could be trusted, audit was pointless. Trust, in other words, was displaced from professionals directly engaged in service delivery to more remote professionals engaged in scrutinizing other professionals. (In the case of the academic profession, the paradox went deeper. Teaching quality was audited by academics. In effect, then, the funding councils to whom the auditors were ultimately responsible were saying that academics could not be trusted to teach properly, but could be trusted to audit other academics.) There was another paradox as well. Professional practices are necessarily opaque, even mysterious, to those outside the profession concerned: professionals are people who have mastered demanding practices which outsiders have not mastered. By definition, then, external audit cannot judge the *quality* of professional performance in the way that members of the relevant profession would do: only teachers know what it is to be a good teacher; only barristers know what it is to be a good advocate. The implications are disturbing. Since they can't judge quality, external auditors have to construct a proxy for it; and the most convenient proxy is quantity. The 'audit explosion', as Michael Power has called it,[13] was bound to privilege quantitative measurement over qualitative judgement. That was only the beginning. Audit is an iron cage. Once professionals were subjected to external audit, they had to adapt their practices to the demands of the audit process, just as managers in the old Soviet Union had to adapt theirs to the demands of Gosplan. Little by little, they began to lose the autonomy which is fundamental to professionalism. In the process, the professional ethic, which presupposes professional autonomy, lost meaning, while the trust relationships between professionals and clients were endangered. The more professionals were audited, the less professional they were able to be. As Power puts it,

> Instead of involving direct observation, audit is largely an indirect form of 'control of control'. . . . In a number of areas this results in a preoccupation with the auditable process rather than the substance of activities. This in turn burdens the auditee with the need to invest in mechanisms of compliance. . . . Concepts of performance and quality are in danger of being defined largely in terms of conformity to auditable process. . . .
>
> . . . In the process of constructing subjects as responsible auditees local structures of trust are displaced and potentially distorted.[14]

The academic profession was harried unmercifully. Academic tenure was effectively abolished; a clause protecting academic freedom was inserted in the relevant legislation only because enough Conservative peers rebelled against their own Government to carry it in the teeth of ministerial opposition. The academic-dominated University Grants Committee, which had disbursed Government money to the universities since the 1920s, was replaced by a Funding Council, whose policies were determined by the Secretary of State; the statute decreed that the academic members of the Council were to be in a minority. Academic research was audited by a costly and bureaucratic appraisal system of ever-increasing complexity, whose judgements carried substantial financial rewards and penalties with them, and led to a marked increase in the quantity of academic publications, accompanied, many academics believed, by a decline in their quality. The teaching profession fared a little better, but only a little. A centrally determined 'national curriculum' took control over school curricula away from teachers, and gave it to the Secretary of State. Schools were allowed (indeed, encouraged) to 'opt out' of local authority control – which, in practice, meant opting in to central government control. A Local Management of Schools initiative devolved control over budgets to individual schools, forcing them to compete for parental custom in yet another proxy market.

Essentially the same logic governed health policy. On strict neo-liberal assumptions, the National Health Service was, if anything, even more obnoxious than the pre-Thatcher universities and schools. It was unashamedly collectivist, not to say socialist; it was run by professionals whose ethic ran counter to the shibboleths of the free market. Since it was also popular – indeed, the single most popular legacy of the post-war growth of the public domain – the Thatcher governments had to proceed cautiously, 'progressively discrediting, destabilizing and supplanting existing institutions',[15] while shrinking from overt radicalism. After her third election victory, however, Thatcher the crusader got the better of Thatcher the cautious politician. The result was the 1990 National Health Service and Community Care Act creating a so-called internal market, in which providers (in other words, hospitals) were supposed to compete for custom from purchasers (in other words, general practitioners). Most hospitals became allegedly self-governing trusts, whose boards were in fact appointed (and dismissible) by the Secretary of State. The most obvious consequence was an explosive growth in administrative costs and the number of managers. By 1995, administrative costs had increased from 5–6 per cent of total NHS spending to 11 per cent; in one hospital, two administrators had been replaced by twenty-six.[16] Less obvious, but equally significant, were an erosion of medical autonomy, the creation of a mass of quangos, 'remote, secretive and subject to political manipulation',[17] and a marked increase in central control. By comparison, the police had it easy; but even they suffered ever-greater, tighter control from the centre. Elaborate appraisal systems measured police performance against centrally determined targets, while the Government explicitly declared that the purpose of the 1994 Police and Magistrates Courts Act was to 'refocus police priorities and direct them to those things which the *government* considers the police should be tackling'.[18] To drive home the lesson, chief constables were put on fixed-term contracts.

Police authorities remained, but only as pale shadows of their former selves.

In this complex story, two themes stand out: market mimicry and central control. The two are linked. Only the central state could remake civil servants, academics, doctors, schoolteachers, social workers and the rest in the image of the enterprise culture. To do this, the core executive at the apex had to concentrate ever more power in its own hands. One consequence was the rising grovel count in Whitehall and the centrally imposed audits that proliferated throughout the public services. Another was a long and bitter battle between Government at the centre and the local authorities which had once figured in Conservative Party rhetoric as bastions of diversity and freedom. There was a factitious element in this battle. Many big cities were governed by far-left Labour parties which tried unavailingly (and, as it turned out, counter-productively) to use the feeble powers of the 'local state' to protect their constituents from the consequences of central Government's policies. For their pains, their powers were further enfeebled. But that is only part of the story. Populist politics are inescapably centralist. A crusading Prime Minister who saw herself as the incarnation of the undifferentiated national will, and who derived much of her authority from her extraordinary ability to speak directly to the sovereign people, could hardly fail to come into conflict with local authorities that represented particular electorates in particular places.

One of the dominant themes of post-war British history was a steady shift of power from local to central government. The Thatcher governments saw a radical acceleration, amounting to a virtual revolution in the territorial constitution. Local authorities were remorselessly stripped of their functions, and imprisoned in an ever-tighter cage of financial control. In the course of the 1980s, around a fifth of the total number of council houses were sold off to their tenants under the Thatcher Government's so-called Right to Buy legislation. By the end of the decade, the vast majority of new starts were carried out by unelected housing associations, 90 per cent of whose funding came from the Housing Corporation, a national quango, financed by central government. The polytechnics were taken out of local authority hands, and eventually given university status. Opted-out schools competed with local-authority schools. The mere fact that they existed gave the parents and governors of the schools that refrained from opting out a powerful lever with which to challenge local-authority education policy. Where the old local health authorities had included local authority representatives, the new district health authorities had none. In the areas most in need of it, responsibility for urban renewal went to appointed Urban Development Councils, quangos with the power to override local-authority plans. Local councils were compelled to de-regulate bus services, and were forbidden to subsidize public transport. They were also compelled to invite tenders for a wide range of services, including school meals, refuse collection and street cleaning. The metropolitan counties set up by a Conservative Government in 1974 were summarily abolished in 1986. So was the twenty-year-old Greater London Council, the sole London-wide elected authority. Its functions passed to a whole nexus of quangos, dependent on central government.

Journey's End?

Revolutions usually blow themselves out sooner or later. The initial flush of exaltation pales; blissful dawn gives way to a banal afternoon. By the mid-1990s, it looked as if Britain's neo-liberal cultural revolution had conformed to that pattern. Despite remarkable achievements – profound changes in the political and moral economies and, still more perhaps, in the terms of public debate – the revolutionaries seemed exhausted, and bereft of new ideas. The sequel was, in some ways, even more remarkable. To it, I now turn.

5

Counter-Attack

By the late 1990s, it looked as if the neo-liberal crusaders had overreached themselves, provoking a Polanyiesque reaction against free-market fundamentalism. In 1997, Tony Blair, the leader and architect of a born-again 'New' Labour Party, found himself in office, at the head of the most inexperienced Cabinet in modern British history. However, hopes that reborn social democracy would undo the neo-liberal cultural revolution were soon disappointed. The notion that New Labour has invariably followed where the Thatcher and Major governments led is wide of the mark: Blair is not Thatcher in drag. Like their predecessors, he and his colleagues want to use the power of the state to enable Britain to 'adapt' to the imperatives of the global market-place; but they do not want to use it in the same way. They do not believe that, once the cultural and institutional barriers to free competition have been demolished, market forces will do the rest. They want deliberately to improve the stock of human capital, to equip the disadvantaged to compete in an ever more demanding labour market, and, in an eery echo of the nineteenth century, to re-engineer the welfare state so as to favour the deserving and penalize the undeserving; and they believe that this cannot be done without extensive public intervention and modest redistribution. (They have also introduced a minimum wage, countervailing, albeit only slightly, the forces at work in the labour market.) All this, they assume, entails a still more powerful central state, with a still more intrusive Treasury at its heart.

Paradoxically, moreover, power hogging has gone hand in hand with a degree of power shedding. Between them, devolution for Scotland and Wales, subtle and far-reaching changes in the always distinctive governance of Northern Ireland, abolition of the voting rights of most (though not all) hereditary peers, an Act protecting human rights, proportional representation for European Parliament elections and the devolved assemblies created by the devolution statutes, and a directly elected mayor of London have transformed the British Constitution, in a way that would have been unthinkable under the Thatcher and Major governments. As I tried to show in my account of the Government's feud with Ken Livingstone, ministers have sometimes displayed a revealing mixture of exasperation and disdain when local leaders and electorates have tried to use the powers which decentralization has put into their hands. Moreover, there is less to the devolution statutes than meets the eye; the authorities they have created are still financed by grants from central government, so the purse-strings are still held in London. Still, there is no doubt that New Labour's constitutional changes have weakened the centre's capacity to have its own way. Some of them have also strengthened the public domain. As its title implies, the Human Rights Act has fortified citizenship rights against the state; with all their weaknesses, the devolution statutes have created new possibilities for civic engagement.

For the most part, however, Blair and his colleagues have followed the previous regime's approach to the public domain. There are echoes of Gladstone's second commandment in his insistence that rights imply duties, and in his Government's attempts to combat social exclusion; but measures to protect the public domain from further incursions by the market domain or to roll back the incursions of the 1980s and early 1990s are conspicuous by their absence. Instead, New Labour has pushed marketization and privatization forward, at least as zealously as the Conservatives did, narrowing the frontiers of the public domain in the process. The new regime is no more friendly to professionals than the old one was, and, like the old one, it sees the professional ethic as a camouflage for vested interests, resisting attempts to make them accountable. Though it sometimes talks the language of community, it refuses to acknowledge that community loyalties can be forged only in a social realm protected from market power. Ministerial rhetoric is saturated with the language of consumerism. The public services are to be 'customer focused'; schools and colleges are to ensure that 'what is on offer responds to the needs of consumers'; the 'progressive project' is to be subjected to 'rebranding'.[1] As all this implies, the *kulturkampf* described in the last chapter succeeded in its central aim. Neo-liberal political economy has become part of the mental furniture of the political elite – in part, of course, because it runs with the grain of the world's capital markets, and echoes the assumptions of the institutions of global economic governance; in part because many, if not most, of the institutions and practices which used to protect the public domain from market incursions were destroyed in the Thatcher and Major years. Like their predecessors, Blair and his ministers have internalized the axioms of the capitalist renaisssance of our time: privatization, de-regulation, free trade, low taxation, budgetary orthodoxy. These define the limits within which their domestic policies are framed. When they say they are new, they mean that they have abandoned the old social-democratic dream of mastering or remodelling capitalism. They also mean that the new global economic order is an iron cage, to which all governments and societies must adapt; and that the hyper-individualistic Anglo-American version of capitalism offers the only route to adaptation. Albeit with different emphases and some qualifications, the neo-liberal revolution continues.

By the same token, New Labour's approach to leadership and governance mimics its predecessors'. Like Thatcher, but more skilfully, Blair has sought to speak directly to an undifferentiated 'people', over the heads of the intermediate institutions in which the values and practices of the public domain were once embedded. In some respects his populism goes further than hers. Though she had nothing but contempt for the trade unions, the local authorities, the universities and the old-style civil service, there was one intermediate institution for which Thatcher had a profound, ingrained respect. She embodied the culture and instincts of the Conservative Party more thoroughly than any other post-war leader. By contrast, Blair's disdain for his party – indeed, for party as such – is almost palpable. As he sees it, New Labour is barely a party at all. It is a personal vehicle for his own history-less, free-floating secular ecumenism and moral unction, which he can steer in any direction he likes. From it, he can address the suburbs as well as the inner cities, rich as well as poor, old as well as young, Christians as well as unbelievers, hunters as well as animal-rights activists, supporters of family values as well as campaigners for gay rights. His Big Tent shelters all men and women of good will, excluding only incorrigible opponents of the 'permanent revolution' of the Third Way.[2]

This does not mean that he always listens to the people, still less that he feels bound to do what they want. The story of the London Underground showed that. So, much more dramatically, did his disdain for public opinion during the run-up to the Iraq War. But populist leaders often disdain the opinions of the people they claim to represent. Like most populists, Blair has constructed an imaginary people in his own image, and it is to and for this imaginary people that he speaks. He assumes that if real people disagree with him and his imaginary people, they must have failed to understand him. Given time, and a more strenuous effort to convince them of the purity of his motives and the depth of his empathy

with them, they will surely come round. After all, they are
sound at heart; and his motives *are* pure. In any case, the
imaginary people and the real people usually march together.
Whereas populists like William Jennings Bryan and David
Lloyd George had to rely on intuition, Blair and his associates
have made use of sophisticated modern techniques of opinion research to track every shift in the public mood and help
them shape it to suit their purposes. Political leaders have
always tried to present their policies as attractively as they
can. Under Blair, policy making and presentation form a
seamless web.

Blair's populism is no more compatible with the civic
ideal of liberty, diversity and engagement than Thatcher's
was. In a haunting passage in *Democracy in America*
Alexis de Tocqueville warned that democracy was menaced
by a new and subtle kind of despotism, in which an 'im-
mense and tutelary power' drew its authority from popular
election.

> That power is absolute, minute, regular, provident, and mild.
> It would be like the authority of a parent if, like that author-
> ity, its object was to prepare men for manhood; but it seeks,
> on the contrary, to keep them in perpetual childhood: it is
> well content that the people should rejoice, provided they
> think of nothing but rejoicing. For their happiness such a
> government willingly labours, but it chooses to be the sole
> agent and the only arbiter of that happiness. . . . [W]hat
> remains but to spare them all the care of thinking and all the
> trouble of living?
>
> I have always thought that servitude of the regular, quiet,
> and gentle kind which I have just described might be com-
> bined more easily than is commonly believed with some of
> the outward forms of freedom, and that it might even establish
> itself under the wing of the sovereignty of the people.[3]

Thatcher's populism could hardly be described as 'regular,
provident and mild'. The phrase might have been penned
with Blair's in mind.

Intermediate Institutions under Attack

Like Thatcher's, New Labour's populism breeds a pervasive suspicion of the intermediate institutions which are among the most important elements in the public domain, sometimes coupled with an exasperated contempt for their elites. The legal profession, the courts, and the cultural and ideological underpinnings of civil liberty are favourite targets. David Blunkett, Blair's second Home Secretary, has made a speciality of attacking 'triumphalist' lawyers, 'airy-fairy libertarians', 'bleeding heart liberals', and judges who do not 'live in the real world'. Under the banner of 're-balancing' the criminal justice system, he and his immediate predecessor, Jack Straw, have made strenuous efforts to limit the discretion of the judiciary, to curtail the rights of accused persons, to give more power to the Home Office and the police, and, in general, to strengthen the state's capacities for surveillance. In the process, a crucial building block of the rule of law – the principle that it is better for a guilty person to go free than for an innocent person to be convicted – has been lost to sight.

In a different sphere, devolution to the non-English nations of the United Kingdom (perhaps to be followed by regional government in parts of England) has gone hand in hand with tighter central control over local government. In the name of modernization, ministers have launched a plethora of initiatives, designed to force local councils to dance to the centre's tune. Though 'crude and universal' capping has been abandoned, the Treasury's grip on local-authority finance is as tight as ever. OFSTED (the Office for Standards in Education) has gained new powers at the expense of local education authorities. Action 'zones' have been created 'with reckless abandon',[4] further strengthening the centre at the expense of the localities. As viewed from Whitehall, local authorities exist to deliver centrally determined services to uniform, centrally imposed standards. Their performance is judged by centrally devised audits, and the centre then rewards the successful and punishes the failures. They are puppets dancing on the centre's strings, not vehicles for civic engagement in the localities for which they are supposed to speak.

By early 2003, it is true, there were signs of a change of tone. There was talk of a 'new localism'. In return for 'reform', Chancellor Brown declared in February 2003, the 'best performing localities' would be granted new freedoms and flexibilities, including the removal of revenue and capital ring fencing, and the withdrawal of reserve powers over capping.[5] Eventually, local communities would be able to devise their own performance indicators. On close examination, however, the new localism did not look very local. The new freedoms it promised were to be rewards for centrally judged good behaviour, not rights. Locally devised performance indicators would be added to national targets, creating a new set of hoops for local managers to jump through, without replacing the old ones.

A similar mixture of gingerly decentralization and camouflaged centralism ran through the most controversial manifestation of the new localism – the creation of so-called Foundation Hospitals. These were to be part of the NHS, but they were not to be subject to direction by the Secretary of State. Foundation Trusts would be not-for-profit corporate bodies, owned by 'members' drawn partly from self-selected members of the local community and partly from hospital staff, perhaps with patients and carers included. They would be free to retain surpluses, to invest in new forms of service delivery, to sell land, and to borrow capital, subject to their ability to repay. Each Trust would have a Board of Governors, largely elected by the members, and a Board of Directors chosen by the Governors. Performance would be monitored by a Regulator. However, freedom from detailed ministerial direction did not imply freedom from central control. The strait-jacket of nationally determined targets and league tables that constrained the managers of NHS hospitals would embrace Foundation Hospitals as well. Their borrowings would count towards the total NHS budget, so that the spectre of Treasury control would still loom in the background. Since the lion's share of their income would come from Primary Care Trusts, which *would* be subject to central direction, the Secretary of State would retain a powerful lever with which to influence their policies without assuming responsibility for them. And, while centralism lurked in the background, there was a significant absentee from the localist foreground. Local councils, the elected representatives of the local communities which the Government said it wished to empower, were nowhere mentioned. In some ways, Foundation Trusts seemed likely to strengthen the public domain, at least in the short term. They offered a locally embedded form of social ownership, escaping both the intrusive state and the voracious market. They provided new opportunities for civic engagement. Their long-term implications were not so clear. There was an obvious danger that they might pave the way for a New Labour version of the Conservatives' internal market. A careful listener could not help noticing that the marketizers' mantras – 'choice', 'consumer' and the 'individual' – loomed ominously large in ministerial rhetoric. The NHS, declared Alan Milburn, the then Health Secretary, in the Second Reading debate,

> was formed in the era of the ration book. . . . Today we live in a different world. Whether we like it or not, this is a consumer age. People demand services that are tailored to their individual needs. They want choice and expect quality – we all do it and we all know it. These changes cannot be ignored, they are here to stay and they challenge every one of our great public services.[6]

The great question is how to meet this challenge: how to preserve the values of citizenship and service in the face of consumerist pressures. The Government's answer is a resounding silence.

More generally, the Northcote–Trevelyan doctrine that public administration should be conducted by a disinterested, non-partisan civil service, with a professional ethic and career paths protected from political interference, is as remote from Blairite governance as it was from Thatcherite. Politically appointed special advisers proliferate, particularly at the apex of government in no. 10 Downing Street. (Where John Major's government made do with thirty-eight, Blair's first government had seventy-four.[7]) More significant than the increase in their number is the enhancement of their role. In certain departments, at any rate, unelected special advisers are, to all intents and purposes, policy-makers, with at least as much influence on decisions as junior ministers. On some issues, members of the Prime Minister's Policy Unit, also unelected, are probably as influential as Cabinet ministers, nominally answerable to the House of Commons. One of the first things Blair did when he entered office was to give two political appointees – his press secretary, Alastair Campbell, and his chief of staff, Jonathan Powell – authority over civil servants. (Parliament had no say in this portentous change in Britain's unwritten Constitution, since it was made by Orders in Council – in other words, by using the royal prerogative.) Many top civil service posts have been filled by outsiders from the corporate sector, recruited through open competition. These new entrants may widen the gene pool of Whitehall, but, by definition, they have not been socialized into the professional ethic of the career civil service of the past. They are inherently more dependent on ministerial favour than old-style civil servants used to be, and less eager to preserve the boundaries between the public and market domains: they would not have been recruited in the first place if those boundaries had remained inviolate.

As all this implies, the cult of private-sector managerialism has as many votaries in the Blair Government as it did in Thatcher's or Major's. The trust-denying audit explosion, which the neo-liberal revolutionaries helped to ignite, shows no sign of abating. In universities, schools, hospitals and social service departments, crude performance indicators, simplistic league tables, and centrally imposed targets still undermine professional autonomy and narrow the scope for professional judgement. On a deeper level, Blair and his colleagues share their predecessors' assumption that the private corporate sector offers the sole model for the efficient management of public services. That, of course, was one of the reasons for their adamantine insistence that investment in the infrastructure of the London Underground had to be carried out through a PPP, even if London's electors wanted none of it. Behind their mantra of public-service 'reform' lie the assumptions that the public services should be run, as far as possible, as though they were private firms, and that a mixture of liberally applied sticks and rather meagre carrots will ensure that this happens. Their goals differ from their predecessors', but the mechanisms through which they pursue them are the same. In a word, market mimicry and central control still rule, OK?

At first sight, the aloof, monarchical state of Gladstone's day is a thing of the past. Today's state could scarcely be less aloof. It is a nagging, interfering presence in every corner of social life, imbued with a culture of command and control. The cult of private-sector managerialism and the accompanying audit explosion have transformed the attitudes and behaviour of its managers. In the non-English nations of the United Kingdom, its writ no longer runs as surely as it used to do. But it is still monarchical – one of the reasons why the culture of command and control has taken root so easily. Blair's disdain for the views of the British people at the start of the Iraq War is the grossest manifestation of that culture in living memory, but it is by no means the only one. Ministers at the centre are still the Queen's ministers. Civil servants are still servants of the Crown, not of Parliament or the public. Most of the Crown's extensive prerogative powers are still at the disposal of the Government of the day, enabling the Prime Minister to reconstruct the state machine, without an Act of Parliament, through Orders in Council, and ensuring that the conduct of foreign policy escapes effective parliamentary scrutiny. The monarchical state and the public domain have always been uneasy bedfellows. Under Blair, as under Thatcher, the former now seems bent on undermining the latter.

A Downward Curve

The public domain survives. Despite audits, league tables, politically driven targets, and, in the case of public-sector professionals, salaries which have failed miserably to keep pace with the private sector, social workers, academics, doctors, teachers, consultants, nurses, engineers and the rest mostly do their best to abide by their own particular versions of the professional ethic. The BBC World Service is still the envy of other countries. In the once grimy, dispiriting centres of old industrial cities such as Glasgow, Newcastle and Leeds, vigorous local leaders, often acting in partnership with the private sector, have renewed public spaces and revitalized local economies, sometimes to spectacular effect. Particularly in the fields of environmental protection and human rights, NGOs are ever more active and effective. The National Trust has more than 2.7 million members and donors. The Royal Society for the Protection of Birds has 1,022,000 members, and Amnesty International slightly more than 169,000 in the United Kingdom. Of course, many members of such bodies do little more than sign the occasional cheque. But when great issues are at stake, the sleeping dogs of public engagement sometimes wake up. The million-strong demonstration against the threatened Iraq War that filled the streets of London in February 2003 showed that the civic ideal had more life in it than Blair and his associates can have wished or expected.

Yet these are blips on a downward curve. At the start of the twenty-first century, there is no sign that the institutions, values and practices of the public domain are about to end the long retreat that began in the 1970s. The civic ideal showed remarkable vitality in the weeks before the Iraq war, but it was not vital enough to stop the Prime Minister committing British troops to a war of doubtful legality, opposed by a majority both of the British people and of the UN Security Council. I said a moment ago that professionals of all sorts 'do their best' to abide by the professional ethic, but the combination of market mimicry and central control hems them in so tightly that, all too often, their best is no longer as professional as they would like. Academics can no longer teach or do research in the way their professional judgement dictates. They have to keep one eye (sometimes both eyes) on time-consuming assessment procedures imposed by government-appointed funding councils. The competitive pressures fostered by school league tables distort the judgement of the teaching profession. Hospital consultants have to temper theirs to the fluctuating priorities of a headline-conscious Secretary of State. Under-funding forces public-domain institutions ranging from Oxbridge colleges to football teams, opera companies and even police forces to scrabble for private-sector sponsorships, conveying the subliminal message that market power is, and ought to be, unchallengeable.

That message reinforces (and is in turn reinforced by) the monochrome monism of public debate. Politicians of ambition and ability who aspire to govern the country can no longer afford to challenge the fundamental axioms of the neo-liberal world-view. The only question is how best to give effect to them. To suggest otherwise – to suggest, for example, that income tax should be seen as a badge of citizenship, that de-regulation of the labour market is incompatible with the enrichment of human capital, or even that there is nothing sacrosanct about the Anglo-American model of capitalism – is to court political marginalization. On a deeper level, the notions that the public interest can and should be distinguished from private interests, and that human flourishing depends on satisfying public needs as well as private wants, have virtually disappeared from political argument. When political leaders debate the future of the public services, they do so in the quintessentially *private* perspective of the individual consumer. (Alan Milburn's case for Foundation Hospitals is a revealing example.) The question at issue is how to balance competing private claims – private claims to publicly provided goods, financed through taxation, against private claims to privately provided ones, bought in the market-place. Few dare to make a public-interest argument: to suggest that public expenditure on universities or libraries or old-age pensions or even hospitals enriches the entire society, including those who don't use the services in question as well as those who do, and that a consumerist perspective on the question of how they should be funded is therefore dangerously out of place. The equally crucial notion of democratic citizenship has fared no better. Populist centralism has no place for the civic ideal of open debate and public engagement. In a populist polity, citizenship is hollowed out. The people are passive, not active – consumers of public policy, not participants in shaping it. Their wishes are conveyed to policy-makers through the leader's intuitions or the pollster's focus groups. British politics has not yet reached that position, but it is hard to deny that it is moving in that direction.

Partly as cause, and partly as consequence, public trust in some of the key institutions of the public domain is dribbling away. The process is complex, confused and laden with paradox. The concept of public trust – indeed, of trust as such – is hard to unpack. Fortunately, there is no need to do so here. For the purposes of this book, what matters is that the erosion of public trust has taken place in a way that makes nonsense of the assumptions behind the marketization of the last twenty years. Central to the marketizers' case is the claim that actors in the public domain cannot be trusted to deliver, that the panoply of audits, targets and league tables I have been discussing is essential to keep them on their toes. Yet the public seems to have lost trust in the marketizers more than in the marketized, in the votaries of private-sector managerialism more than in those they scorn. In a 2002 MORI poll, 91 per cent trusted doctors to tell the truth, and only 6 per cent did not. The figures for teachers were 85 per cent and 10 per cent, and for professors 78 per cent and 10 per cent. By contrast, civil servants were trusted by only 45 per cent and distrusted by 42 per cent. Those who trusted business leaders were heavily outnumbered by those who distrusted them (25 per cent to 62 per cent). Government ministers were trusted by 20 per cent and distrusted by 73 per cent.[8] A 1996 study by the Henley Centre told a similar story. Confidence in a wide range of traditional institutions had fallen, but Parliament and the civil service had suffered by far the biggest falls.[9]

At the same time, public disenchantment with government, parties, politicians and the electoral process has grown apace. In 1986 the British Social Attitudes survey asked its sample how far they trusted British governments 'to place the needs of the nation above the interests of their own political party'. Thirty-eight per cent trusted the Government to do this 'just about always' or 'most of the time'; 57 per cent trusted it 'only some of the time' or 'almost never'. By 1996, the Government was trusted by only 22 per cent, and distrusted by 75 per cent. Only 28 per cent trusted civil servants to 'stand firm against a minister who wants to provide false information to Parliament'. A derisory 9 per cent trusted politicians of any party 'to tell the truth when they are in a tight corner'.[10] The figures for 2000 are even more striking. Sixty-six per cent of those surveyed by ICM for the Joseph Rowntree Reform Trust thought the untruthfulness of government ministers was a major problem. Seventy-three per cent thought ministers and their advisory committees could not be trusted to tell the truth about the safety of GM foods and crops. Seventy-four per cent thought they could not be trusted to tell the truth about food safety in general, and 75 per cent that they could not be trusted to tell the truth about the safety of nuclear installations.[11] Disdain for the electoral process was widespread too. By the 1990s, substantial majorities agreed or strongly agreed that MPs soon lost touch with the electorate, and that political parties were 'only interested in people's votes not in their opinions'. Meanwhile, general election turn-out fell sharply. Turn-out in the 1997 election was the lowest since the Second World War. In 2001 it was lower than in any general election since the coming of manhood suffrage in 1918.

Yet interest in politics did not decline,[12] while reported readiness to take part in non-electoral political activities, such as signing a petition, contacting an MP, or going on a protest or demonstration, actually grew. Support for a wide range of constitutional reforms grew as well. By 1996, three-fifths of those polled by the Social Attitudes Survey agreed that British courts should be able 'to overrule parliament on any law which denies people their basic rights', and around 90 per cent supported freedom of information in respect of economic plans and plans for new legislation. That was before the Blair Government's constitutional legislation, but MORI's 2000 poll showed that the public's appetite for reform had grown with feeding. If those who said they 'strongly agreed' and those who said they 'tended to agree' are added together, support for fixed-term Parliaments reached 60 per cent, for a written constitution 71 per cent, and for a Freedom of Information Act 81 per cent. On the same basis, 53 per cent thought Parliament has too little control over the government, and 60 per cent thought government too centralized. Devolution had far more supporters than opponents. Seventy-two per cent of Scots thought the Scottish Parliament and executive should have more power, as against 3 per cent who thought they should have less. The figures for Wales were 44 per cent and 10 per cent; and for London, 44 per cent and 9 per cent. Attitudes to extra-parliamentary forms of political action were remarkably radical. Substantial majorities thought the Seattle and Prague anti-globalization demonstrations, the anti-capitalist street demonstrations in London, the British petrol blockades and the Countryside Alliance and pro-hunting demonstrations were all either 'definitely' or 'perhaps' justified. The key to that apparently undifferentiated disdain for convention lay in the answer to another question. Asked if peaceful protests, blockades and demonstrations were a 'legitimate way of expressing people's concerns' if governments did not listen, 81 per cent either strongly agreed or said they tended to agree. Only a minuscule 3 per cent strongly disagreed.

Two implications stand out. The first is that populist centralism is profoundly unpopular. The picture that emerges from the opinion surveys I have described is not one of cynicism, still less of apathy. It is one of street-wise disaffection. The evidence does not suggest that the British have lost interest in politics, or that they think collective action is invariably a waste of time. The ancient British tradition of extra-parliamentary protest is alive and well. Constitutional reforms designed to devolve power, to protect human rights, and to make the executive more transparent are supported by large majorities. A crushing majority of the British people distrusts the political class, and has lost faith in the system through which it is governed; but that is because the political class increasingly behaves as if it distrusts the people, and because the system no longer offers a choice between alternative visions of the political economy. Public disenchantment is a response to the hollowing out of citizenship, not a cause.

The second implication is bleaker. In principle, at least, the public domain is a space where public questions are publicly debated and resolved, where citizens come together to decide what should count as the public interest and how it should be embodied in public policy – in other words, a space for *politics*. If the political system loses legitimacy, if citizens lose confidence in the institutions that are supposed to represent them and to hold the ring for free and open debate, that space is likely to contract; and once it starts to contract, it is likely to go on doing so. After all, what is the point of debate if no one listens? If debate is pointless, what is the point of citizenship? And if there is no point in citizenship, how can there be a public domain? These questions reverberate through the survey findings I have mentioned. Their clear implication is that public disaffection on its current scale poses a growing threat to the public domain, and to all that it means for personal fulfilment and social well-being.

Towards a New Public Philosophy

The threats to the public domain feed on themselves. The audit explosion is an obvious example. Auditors are called in because auditees are assumed to be unreliable. But once the audit train leaves the station, it becomes self-contradictory to jump off: if auditees perform properly only when they are audited, repeated audits are the only way to ensure that proper performance continues. The auditors' 'rituals of verification'[13] are self-validating and self-perpetuating. The same applies to the miasma of distrust that now envelops the political elite. The more the public distrusts politicians, the more the media will cater to its distrust, the more the public will feel that its lack of trust is justified, the more politicians will distrust the public, and the more the space for democratic politics will contract. Marketization is self-reinforcing too, and with even more damaging results. The restless search for profit that drives capitalist economies (and gives them their amazing dynamism) is as fundamental to the market domain of the twenty-first century as it was 150 years ago; if the market imperialism it generates is allowed to annex one part of the public domain, it becomes more and more difficult to resist further annexations. Yet, as the radicals of nineteenth-century Britain understood, a public domain protected from market power is a pre-condition of democratic governance. As Tawney pointed out, citizenship rights are, by definition, equal, and market rewards, by definition, unequal. Unless the public domain of citizenship rights is ring-fenced from the market domain of buyers and sellers, the primordial democratic promise of equal citizenship will be negated. Money talks; and the louder it talks, the harder it becomes to hear un-monied voices. Who can doubt that it has talked ever more loudly in the last thirty years?

It is time for a counter-attack. It cannot be a repeat performance of the nineteenth-century counter-movement against market utopianism that Polanyi analysed so memorably. To be sure, there are striking parallels between the state-imposed *laissez-faire* of the early nineteenth century and the state-led neo-liberal revolution of our own day. The 'Old Corruption' that Gladstone and his colleagues sought to extirpate is not a million miles away from the croneyism and clientelism spawned by the new privatism of the last quarter of a century. Money talked as loudly in the nineteenth century as it does today. But despite Gladstone's uncanny skill at mobilizing a popular constituency, and Joe Chamberlain's less skilful attempts to emulate him, populist governance in the style of Thatcher and Blair was unknown in nineteenth-century Britain. (However, there are parallels between both of them and Louis Napoleon, the grave-digger of the second French Republic.) The fragmentation of the professional culture, which has done so much to discredit professionalism and the professional ethic, did not start until the second half of the twentieth century. The state of the early twenty-first century is incomparably bigger, more centralized and more complex than that of the late nineteenth, and modern methods of communication have given it enormously greater capacities for surveillance and control. (It is hard to believe that the audit explosion could have taken place before the advent of the microchip.)

On a different, but equally important level, nineteenth-century Britain was the centre of the greatest empire the world has ever seen, and the linchpin of the world's first global market. Though Victorian policy-makers had to abide by the rules of that market, these were, in the last resort, *British* rules. They were not incarnated in global institutions, preponderantly influenced by a foreign superpower. Most important of all, perhaps, the Victorian architects of the public domain did not have to contend with pervasive public disaffection from the political elite and the political process. Ireland always excepted, Britain's was a remarkably deferential society, presided over by the most relaxed and confident governing class in Europe. Radicals wanted to widen the boundaries of the political nation and make the civic ideal more effective, but their only complaint against the political process was that too many people were excluded from it.

Yet there are lessons to be learned from the nineteenth century. Though they did not use the term, the Victorians invented the public domain. Now it has to be reinvented. Its boundaries will have to be re-established, and they will have to be equipped with new barriers against incursions from the private and market domains. As in nineteenth-century Britain, it will need a lot of creativity, imagination and flexibility to do this, and it will almost certainly take a long time. As in nineteenth-century Britain, success will depend on a mixture of state intervention, initiatives by charities, NGOs, trade unions, mutuals and other voluntary associations, and action by local authorities, probably with voluntary bodies and local authorities in the lead. Private firms committed to the public interest may contribute as well: as I suggested in chapter 1, the public domain must not be confused with the public sector. Most of all, it will depend on a cultural shift comparable to the shift that Gladstone described in his *Nineteenth Century* article. That, in turn, will depend on the development of a public philosophy capable of answering the now-entrenched orthodoxies of neo-liberalism, of challenging the all-pervasive ideology of consumerism, and of mobilizing the public conscience in the way that the champions of the public domain mobilized it in the nineteenth and early twentieth centuries.

Thirteen simple propositions would form the core of such a philosophy:

1   A vigorous and extensive public domain is fundamental to a civilized society, to crucially important forms of human flourishing, and, not least, to democratic citizenship.
2   Belief in the possibility of a public interest, distinct from private interests, is fundamental to the public domain. So is a public discourse based on that belief.

3   In the public domain, citizenship rights trump both market power and the ties of family, friendship, neighbourhood and connection.

4   The public domain is, in a special sense, the domain of trust. Trust relationships are fundamental to it; public trust is symbiotically connected with the contestations, debates and negotiations, and the values of equity and citizenship, which are of its essence.

5   It follows that the public domain must be protected from the ever present threat of incursion by the market and private domains.

6   In our time, the chief vehicles for market incursion are the pervasive notion that public domain institutions should be managed as though they were market institutions, and the rhetoric of consumerism.

7   The rule of law, embodied in an independent, authoritative judiciary, and a disinterested, non-partisan professional civil service, have crucial parts to play in protecting the public domain from such incursions.

8   The goods of the public domain must not be treated as commodities or surrogate commodities. Performance indicators designed to mimic the indicators of the market domain are therefore out of place in the public domain, and do more harm than good.

9   By the same token, the language of buyer and seller, producer and consumer, does not belong in the public domain; nor do the relationships which this language implies. People are consumers only in the market domain; in the public domain, they are citizens. Attempts to force these relationships into a market mould undermine the service ethic which is the true guarantor of quality in the public domain. In doing so, they impoverish the entire society.

10 The search for competitiveness – in practice, for higher productivity, achieved by substituting capital for labour – which is proper to the market domain is also out of place in the public domain.

11 Professions, professionalism and the professional ethic are inextricably linked to the public domain. This is most obviously true of public-sector professions, which serve the public interest by definition; but it is also true of private-sector professionals, whose duty is to serve the wider public interest as well as the private interests of their own clients.

12 To carry out their duties, professionals must have the autonomy to exercise their judgement as they see fit. This means that professional performance cannot be assessed, or professional career prospects determined, solely or even mainly by market criteria or criteria that mimic those of the market-place.

13 Wrongly used, state power can do as much damage to the public domain as market power. To guard against that danger, constitutional checks and balances supported by strong and vigorous intermediate institutions, standing between the state and the individual, are indispensable.

Letting Go

Could such a philosophy fly in the real world of the early twenty-first century? What might flight entail? No single person can give definitive answers to these questions. The counter-attack against the market imperialism of our day will not follow a master plan any more than the counter-movement of the late nineteenth century did. Here, I can only sketch a broad approach, as a contribution to debate.

Almost by definition, the philosophy I have described has implications for the outside world as well as for Britain. The *kulturkampf* I described in the last chapter was the local, British version of a world-wide neo-liberal revival which has left its impress on virtually all national political economies – and, for that matter, on the institutions of global economic governance. That revival is both child and parent of the accelerating globalization of the final decades of the last century. The obvious question is whether these world-wide forces can be countervailed, or at least mitigated. It is not an easy one to answer; and in any case a full answer would need another book. Here I can offer only a brief sketch of the way in which I think the question should be approached. Simplifying grossly, the globalization of our day is not as novel as it sometimes looks. Despite important differences, it has much in common with the globalization of the second half of the nineteenth century. The pivot on which nineteenth-century globalization turned was the hegemonic power of that era: namely, the British Empire. The pivot of its twenty-first-century successor is the United States. As a result, it is all too easy to confuse globalization with Americanization. The two are linked, but they are not the same. The former is inescapable; the latter is not bound to be. Of course, no single nation-state can challenge American hegemony, but it does not follow that it is inherently unchallengeable. The European Union has the strength, and may develop the will, to become an alternative pole of power. Meanwhile, a global public space, inhabited by a wide range of global political actors, is beginning tentatively to emerge. Potentially, these are the growth points of a new, multipolar global order, underpinned by a global jurisprudence. Reinventing Britain's public domain and fostering these global growth points are different sides of the same coin.

That said, it would be a counsel of despair to imagine that nothing can be done to reinvent the local, British public domain until such a new order is in place; and in the rest of this chapter I shall focus on Britain. I suggested a moment ago that the public domain cannot be reinvented without a profound cultural shift. Cultures are embodied in, and transmitted by, institutions. Only institutions can keep market imperialism and private favouritism at bay. The neo-liberal revolutionaries sought, quite explicitly, to encourage market imperialism; to that end, they did their best to weaken, intimidate or refashion the institutions that protected the public domain from market power. These institutions must be rebuilt, but it would be fatal to stick to the designs of their original architects. The neo-liberals gave the wrong answer, but they asked the right question. They saw that, in practice, the institutions of the public domain increasingly flouted the civic ideal, that accountability was lacking, that Voice was ineffective. Their mistake was to rely on Exit instead; and that mistake has cost us dearly. The last twenty-five years have taught us that market routes to accountability have no place in the public domain: that attempts to force its institutions to mimic those of the market-place merely degrade them. However, that does not imply a return to the public domain of old days. As I tried to show in chapter 3, its foundations were beginning to crumble when the neo-liberals were still a marginal minority.

The always latent contradiction between the monarchical state and the civic ideal was becoming apparent forty years ago, and it was already beginning to erode public confidence in the political class and the political process. Meanwhile, the arrogance, hermeticism and technocratic aloofness of the elites on which the public domain depended were beginning to alienate the public (or publics) in whose name they acted. Well before that, governments at the centre had started to curtail the autonomy of the local authorities which had once spearheaded the growth of the public domain, and in doing so, to narrow the scope for participation and engagement. Two lessons emerge from the history of the last thirty years. The first is that the public domain cannot be reinvented without halting and then undoing the neo-liberal revolution. The second is that it is equally necessary to make sure that the failings that undermined it in the second half of the twentieth century, and gave the neo-liberals their opportunity, do not reappear.

Two implications stand out. The first is straightforward. It has to do with the dilemma of accountability, which, in one guise or another, has haunted the story I have tried to tell in this book. The search for accountability through Exit has been a disaster for the public domain, and therefore for society at large, but even in its great days, Voice spoke in increasingly feeble, not to say strangulated, tones. The obvious moral is that, if the public domain is to be reinvented, accountability through Voice must be made to work. The second implication is more complex. The chief carriers of the continuing neo-liberal revolution (and the chief enemies of the civic ideal) are market mimicry, populist governance and central control. These are linked. Market mimicry has been imposed on the institutions of the public domain by the control-hungry core executive at the heart of the central state. The imagined people's will, evoked and focused by the populist leader, legitimates central control and gives the would-be controllers a powerful psychic boost. Central control is the prize for which populist leaders yearn. Behind all three stand the monarchical state and the tradition of autonomous executive power it embodies. In the days of Gladstone and Joe Chamberlain, when the public domain was taking shape, the state was aloof as well as monarchical, and it treated intermediate institutions with benign neglect. But those days have gone. Now intermediate institutions are targets for marketizers, populists and central controllers alike – for marketizers because they impede marketization, for populists because they clog up the channels that link the people to the leader, for central controllers because they challenge their authority – and the nagging, interfering, omnipresent monarchical state does its best to hobble, undermine and discredit them. Once again there is an obvious moral. If the public domain is to be reinvented, the monarchical state must be disinvented.

Disinventing the Monarchical State

The question is, how? What would accountability through Voice mean for a complex early-twenty-first-century polity? What should a non-monarchical state look like, and how might it take shape? I offer three answers (or sets of answers). The first has to do with attitudes, assumptions and culture. There is an extraordinary paradox about the continuing neo-liberal revolution. 'Adaptation', 'modernization', 'change' are its holy trinity. The revolutionaries endlessly insist that the past must not be allowed to stand in the way of the future. Old habits, old practices, old traditions, old ways of life must be ruthlessly jettisoned if they conflict with the imperatives of modernization, which in practice bear an uncanny resemblance to the imperatives of the global market-place. Only central control can ensure that they *are* jettisoned, with sufficient ruthlessness. Yet, if the history of the last century has one sure lesson, it is that change imposed from the top, measured and policed by procedures contrived at the top, rarely produces the desired results. Command and control destroyed the Soviet Union, inflicted untold damage on Mao's China, and went badly adrift during the post-war Labour Government's planning phase.

Not surprisingly. If change is to stick, it must, in management jargon, be 'owned' by those affected by it. 'Ownership' is impossible without understanding; and understanding has to be built on wide-ranging, uninhibited discussion of the sort that command and control rules out. With part of their minds, the revolutionaries know this. Past failures of central control loom large in their rhetoric. The paradox is that they are themselves imprisoned in the culture of the monarchical state to which central control is now second nature. If the public domain is to be reinvented, and the public philosophy I sketched out a moment ago made to fly, the core executive at the heart of the state must be willing to let go. It must learn a new approach to governance – an approach based on the notion of social learning, in which 'key participants in the policy process . . . come together for discussion and debate'.[14] This does not imply state abdication. It implies that the state ceases to be a commander or a controller, and becomes a learner along with other learners – and, of course, a teacher along with other teachers. Another way of saying the same thing is that the monarchical culture of government at the centre should be replaced with a republican one.

The second answer to the 'how' questions I posed a moment ago is closely related to the first. Social learning implies diversity, pluralism, *difference*. (It would be hard to stay awake, let alone to learn anything, in a class consisting of the teacher's clones.) Differences need protection. Pressures for centralization are omnipresent; and they have been enhanced, not weakened, by the communications revolution. The central state can always find good reasons for arrogating power to itself – social justice, say, or economic efficiency, or public safety in the 'war' against terrorism. All governments – even governments of pluralistic liberals – have a built-in propensity for self-aggrandizement and uniformity. The only way to curb that propensity is to create alternative power centres. As James Madison once put it, 'ambition must be made to counter ambition'. The best defence against the arrogance of power is power. Self-confident and powerful intermediate institutions – local and regional authorities, universities, trade unions, professions, NGOs, the judiciary and the rest – are needed, not just to protect the public domain from market and private power, but also to protect it from an inherently over-intrusive central state.

Letting go would entail an end to the war which the Thatcher, Major and Blair governments have waged against such institutions. Instead of harassing the professions, a government committed to reinventing the public domain would respect and nurture them. Instead of denigrating the professional ethic, and doing its best to whittle professional autonomy away, it would work with the grain of professionalism, and accept that professionals cannot serve the public interest properly unless they have the space in which to exercise their skills in accordance with their professional judgement. It would also recognize that professionals must be accountable to the public, and acknowledge that in the heyday of the public domain, around the middle of the last century, accountability was often lacking. However, it would

approach the thorny problem of how to reconcile accountability with autonomy in a modest, flexible and experimental
spirit. It would abandon the suspicious and impatient hector-
ing and the relentless paper chasing which have done even
more to demoralize public-sector professionals than under-
funding. It would cease to rely on crude, mechanistic and
centrally imposed targets and audits which cannot capture
the subtleties of real-world professional practice, and experiment with subtler, qualitative, more specific and more local
forms of accountability, based on open-ended dialogue
between professionals and their stakeholders.[15] Doctors,
patients, carers, NHS auxiliaries, local councillors and MPs
might consult together over the forms of accountability
best fitted to reconcile the demands of professional medical
autonomy with local needs and priorities. Universities might
involve parents, students and employers, as well as the
Government's Funding Councils, in determining the criteria
and methods by which academic performance should be
assessed. Schools might widen Parent Teacher Associations
to include other stakeholders, to do the same for teaching
performance. Citizens' juries would probably be widely used,
particularly to resolve disputes between stakeholders. But the
details matter less than the approach. The crucial point
is that the watchwords of the new accountability would be
locality, particularity, flexibility and inclusion.

Last, but not least, such a government would adopt a new
approach to central–local relations. Instead of treating local
government as an instrument for delivering policies made at
the centre, it would recognize that different localities are
bound to have different priorities, and rejoice in the opportunities for policy experimentation and civic participation
that such a recognition would bring. (It would also give local
authorities sufficient taxing powers to finance their expend-
itures out of their own resources.) In place of the centralism
which has shaped Whitehall's approach to the territorial
constitution since the First World War, it would, in short,
put the Christian Democratic principle of subsidiarity – the

principle that decisions on public policy should always be taken at the lowest practicable level of government.

The third set of answers to the question of how to disinvent the monarchical state comes into the story at this point. Subsidiarity is indispensable, but it is not enough. Given political imagination and flair, vigorous local and regional authorities, with their own sources of finance, might countervail the power of the central state and develop alternatives to the reigning orthodoxies. This has already happened, to some degree, in Scotland, despite its lack of financial autonomy; and it is not difficult to imagine the same thing happening in the north of England. But, so long as the central state retains its existing form, and the core executive its existing assumptions, the scope for subsidiarity will be limited. Almost by definition, profound changes at the centre will be needed as well.

Not surprisingly, the chief candidates for change are all hangovers from a more or less distant past. The most obvious of them is the House of Lords. It is now an almost entirely nominated body. As such, it has more legitimacy than the largely hereditary upper house used to have; because of this, it is a slightly more effective check on the inevitable self-aggrandizement of the central executive. However, a nominated House can never be legitimate or effective enough to meet the needs of a regime committed to subsidiarity and social learning. Only an upper house endowed with the legitimacy that comes from democratic election can provide an adequate check on the power-hungry central executive. Another obvious candidate is the electoral system. This too is a hangover, though a much less venerable one. First-past-the-post elections and the single-party governments they engender are symbiotically connected with the populist centralism of the last quarter of a century. Proportional representation, and the coalition building it would entail, would not, in itself, create a check on the over-mighty central executive, but it would certainly be a stumbling block for would-be elective dictators.

The third candidate is the post-Thatcher (and post-Northcote–Trevelyan) civil service. The ethic of professionalism and public service that became part of the culture of British public administration during the second half of the nineteenth century has been badly battered for more than twenty years. Individual civil servants may still adhere to it, but it is no longer the lodestar of the civil service as an institution. Because of this, it is no longer axiomatic that senior civil servants are the guarantors of the public domain. One reason is that they are as affected by the pervasive climate of consumerism and neo-liberalism as the rest of the society to which they belong. This is not the whole story, however. At least as important are a built-in tension in the relationship between civil servants and ministers, and a profound ambiguity in the duties that civil servants are meant to discharge. Civil servants are supposed to pursue the public interest. They are also supposed to be servants of the Crown. The notion of 'the Crown' is slippery and in many ways ambiguous, and constitutional authorities differ about its meaning. However, Whitehall orthodoxy is clear. As the then Cabinet Secretary Sir Robert Armstrong put it in a famous memorandum in 1985, 'For all practical purposes, the Crown in this context means and is represented by the Government of the day. . . . The Civil Service as such has no constitutional personality or responsibility separate from the duly constituted Government of the day.'[16]

For the best part of 150 years, duty to what might be called the 'Armstrong Crown' – to the Crown as a synonym for the Government of the day – normally marched in step with duty to the public. With fairly rare exceptions, ministers and civil servants normally respected the public-service ethic and the practices in which it was embedded. (In the appeasement years before the Second World War, and during the Suez crisis in 1956, some civil servants were torn between their duty to the 'Armstrong Crown' and their duty to the public, as they saw it, but the crises of conscience that resulted were exceptional.) The neo-liberal cultural revolution, the new privatism, and the rising 'grovel count' that Lord Bancroft detected have changed all that. Governments no longer respect the public-service ethic of the past; on the contrary, they have tried deliberately to break its hold on the mentality of Whitehall. To that end, they have done their best to reconstruct the civil service in the image of the corporate sector, and to blur the distinction between personal appointees and professional officials – in the process drying up the soil in which the public-service ethic flowered.

Civil servants still serve the 'Armstrong Crown', but it is no longer safe to assume that they pursue the public interest in doing so: perhaps the most startling moral of the Scott Report was that civil servants, as well as ministers, illegitimately equated the public interest with executive convenience. Meanwhile, public trust in civil servants has plummeted, as I mentioned earlier. One of the first steps towards a reinvented public domain is to reinvent the 'Northcote–Trevelyan' ethic of disinterested professionalism and public service, and to embed it once again in the *practice* of British public administration. This is not the place for a thorough examination of all the implications, but one of them is clear. It is not enough to rely on informal usages and inherited assumptions, as the civil servants (and, for that matter, the ministers) of old days could safely do. The role, duties and norms of the civil service must be explicitly laid down in statute, as the Commons Select Committee on Administration has recently suggested; the distinction between political appointees and professional civil servants must be spelled out; candidates for political appointments must be subject to public scrutiny by a parliamentary committee; and their numbers must be rigorously limited. Above all, civil servants must become, in law, servants of Parliament – the representative of the public whose interest they are supposed to pursue – and not of the Crown.

Against that background, the third candidate for change selects itself. At the heart of Britain's monarchical state lie the Crown and the array of precedents, practices and doctrines

covered by the blanket term 'Royal Prerogative'. The
prerogative powers are not all of a piece. Some would belong
to the head of state in a parliamentary republic. But a
wide range of prerogative powers gives executive authority
to ministers; and these help to give the monarchical state its
special character. Rodney Brazier's description is illuminating,
and in some ways chilling.

> If this country has prime ministerial government, it is based
> on the Prime Minister's personal authority which . . . is rooted
> in the prerogative. His right to appoint to the government
> whomsoever he pleases (subject to limited exceptions) reflects
> the legal position that ministers are appointed and hold office
> at the pleasure of the Crown. . . . The prime minister, in his
> capacity as Minister for the civil service, exercises a range of
> authority over the entire public service. This rests primarily
> on the royal prerogative. . . . In the vast bulk of the honours
> system, the Queen's prerogative has been acquired by the
> Prime Minister for his own purposes. The Prime Minister has
> a role to play in ecclesiastical appointments, and he has many
> other general patronage powers. Thus the Chairman and
> Governors of the BBC, the Governor and the directors of the
> Bank of England, the Comptroller and Auditor-General, the
> Parliamentary Commissioner for Administration, the Chair-
> man of the Public Accounts Committee, the Regius Professors,
> and chairmen and members of Royal Commissions and other
> inquiries, and many others, are all appointed by or on behalf
> of the Prime Minister, in general by prerogative acts. . . .
> . . . If a chief officer of police thought that his officers could
> not deal with a serious threat to public order, even if supple-
> mented by police from other areas, he could consult the Home
> Office with a view to troops being sent to help. Ministers
> might then decide to sanction the use of troops under the
> prerogative to help to keep or to restore the peace. . . . Through
> the exercise of prerogative powers Home Office Ministers can
> issue, refuse, impound, and revoke passports, which remain
> the property of the Crown. . . .
> . . . The prerogative gives the government a remarkably free
> hand to conclude treaties: according to British constitutional

practice, Parliament has no formal role in treaty-making, save where a treaty requires a change in English law or the grant of public money, when Parliament will be asked to approve the necessary legislation. Otherwise, Parliament can only express any disapproval of an international agreement through political pressure, or through a formal vote of no confidence. . . .

. . . The recognition of a country as an independent state is effected under the prerogative, as is the decision as to what dealings (if any) should take place between Her Majesty's Government and a regime which has come to power unconstitutionally in another country. The appointment of British Ambassadors and High Commissioners (and in cases where diplomatic relations break down their withdrawal) are effected under the prerogative. . . .

. . . The Suez canal, the Falkland Islands and the Gulf all received British armed forces on ministerial orders under the prerogative power to deploy those forces as the Crown sees fit. . . . The use of British forces in peacekeeping duties abroad flows from the same prerogative basis. The maintenance and organization of the armed forces is still dependent in part on the royal prerogative. The Royal Navy exists by virtue of it. . . . Prerogative is still the basis for the commissioning of officers in all three services; and pay and pensions are determined by royal warrants under it.[17]

In principle, ministers are responsible to Parliament for the way in which they exercise these powers, just as they are for all other executive acts; but ministerial responsibility to Parliament notoriously provides a scanty check on the abuse of executive power. In practice, executive actions under the royal prerogative normally escape parliamentary scrutiny; and many of them are also outside the scope of judicial review. The Prime Minister's conduct as dispenser of patronage and overseer of the civil service; the Home Secretary's conduct as ultimate keeper of the peace; the day-to-day conduct of foreign policy are all hidden by an archaic veil of mystery which Parliament and the courts can hardly penetrate. Some prerogative powers are exorbitant in any case (the monstrous edifice of prime ministerial patronage is the best example). Others are, in themselves, unobjectionable. But a Government committed to public accountability and a reinvented public domain would give them all statutory form, spelling out how and when they could be used, and providing safeguards against misuse.

Taken together, the institutional changes I have suggested would amount to a new constitutional settlement. Such a settlement could be procured piecemeal, one step at a time, in characteristic British fashion. That would be better than nothing. The trouble with piecemeal change, however, is that the expected later steps sometimes fail to follow the earlier ones, and even when they do, the underlying logic and overarching purpose of the whole exercise are not always clear. The barriers that once protected the public domain from the market and private domains grew up piecemeal, but it does not follow that they can be renewed in the same way. In the twenty-first century, the inexplicit, half-conscious incrementalism of the late nineteenth century is unlikely to be enough. The old Constitution – the Constitution that embodied and legitimized the British tradition of autonomous executive power – has collapsed, leaving behind a vacuum of understanding and rhetoric which is the chief (though not the only) begetter of the populist centralism of Thatcher and Blair. In the villages of Westminster and Whitehall, the suggestion that it should be comprehensively recast, in accordance with an explicit set of principles derived from a twenty-first-century version of the civic ideal, may seem startling, or even ridiculous. Yet nothing less will suffice.

Notes

Prologue

1 Preface to 1938 edition of *Equality*, repr. in David Riesman (ed.), *Theories of the Mixed Economy* (William Pickering, London, 1994), p. 15.

2 Colin Leys, *Market-Driven Politics, Neoliberal Democracy and the Public Interest* (Verso, London and New York, 2001).

Chapter 1 Economical with the *Actualité*

1 My account is based on Richard Norton-Taylor, Mark Lloyd and Stephen Cook, *Knee Deep in Dishonour: The Scott Report and its Aftermath* (Victor Gollancz, London, 1996); *Public Law*, special issue on the Scott Report, 1996; Brian Thompson and F. F. Ridley, *Under the Scott-Light: British Government Seen through the Scott Report* (Oxford University Press, Oxford, 1997); and *Report of the Inquiry into the Export of Defence Equipment and Dual-Use Goods to Iraq and Related Prosecutions*, by the Rt. Hon. Sir Richard Scott, the Vice-Chancellor (the Scott Report) (HMSO, London, 1996).

2 Scott Report, para. G17.29.

3 Scott Report, paras D4.1–D4.63.

4 Ibid., para. D4.42.

5   See *Report, Evidence and Supporting Papers of the Inquiry into the Emergence and Identification of Bovine Spongiform Encephalopathy (BSE) and Variant Creutzfeldt–Jakob Disease (vCJD) and the Action Taken in Response to it up to 20 March 1966* (the Phillips Report) (HMSO, London, October 2000), vol. 1. My account of the BSE affair is based on this, and also on Robert J. Maxwell, *An Unplayable Hand? BSE, CJD and the British Government* (King's Fund, London, 1997); Rosalind M. Ridley and Harry F. Baker, *Fatal Protein: The Story of CJD, BSE and Other Prion Diseases* (Oxford University Press, Oxford, 1998).

6   Phillips Report, p. 30.

7   Ibid., pp. 148–50.

8   Ibid., pp. 233–64.

9   Ibid., p. 233.

10 Maxwell, *An Unplayable Hand?*, p. 34.

11 Phillips Report, p. 265.

12 The Phillips Inquiry found that 'it was not MAFF's policy to lean in favour of the agricultural producers to the detriment of the consumer' (see p. xviii). That, of course, is a matter of judgement. In my view, the evidence published in the Report makes clear that, whatever MAFF's *policy* may have been, its judgement was in practice biased by its concern for producer interests.

13 Mark D'Arcy and Rory Maclean, *Nightmare: The Race to Become London's Mayor* (Politicos, London, 2000), p. 52.

14 Ibid., p. 136.

15 Christian Wolmar, *Down the Tube: The Battle for London's Underground* (Aurum Press, London, 2002), pp. 94–5. My account of the dispute over the Underground is based on Wolmar's. See also *The London Underground Public Private Partnership: An Independent Review* (The Industrial Society, London, 2000), and Ben Pimlott and Nirmala Rao, *Governing London* (Oxford University Press, Oxford, 2002).

16 The term is Christian Wolmar's: *Down the Tube*, ch. 7.

17 *London Underground Public Private Partnership*, p. 136.

18 W. H. Greenleaf, *The British Political Tradition*, vol. 1: *The Rise of Collectivism* (Methuen, London, 1983), p. 33.

19 T. H. Marshall, *Citizenship and Social Class and Other Essays* (Cambridge University Press, Cambridge, 1950), p. 56.

20 Ralph Dahrendorf et al., *Report on Wealth Creation and Social Cohesion in a Free Society* (London, 1995), p. 39.
21 In *The Economic Consequences of Mr Churchill*, quoted in D. E. Moggridge, *Maynard Keynes: An Economist's Biography* (Routledge, London and New York, 1992), p. 433.
22 Philip Bobbitt, *The Shield of Achilles: War, Peace and the Course of History* (Penguin Books, London, 2003), pp. 95–143.
23 Michael Walzer, *Spheres of Justice: A Defence of Pluralism and Equality* (Basic Books, New York, 1983).

Chapter 2   The Public Conscience

1 Quoted in H. C. G. Matthew, *Gladstone 1875–1898* (Clarendon Press, Oxford, 1995), p. 85.
2 E. P. Thompson, *Whigs and Hunters: The Origins of the Black Acts* (Allen Lane, London, 1975), p. 264.
3 Harold Perkin, *The Origins of Modern English Society 1780–1880*, paperback edition (Routledge & Kegan Paul, London, 1972).
4 Karl Polanyi, *The Great Transformation: The Political and Economic Origins of our Time* (Beacon paperback edition, Boston, 1957).
5 Ibid., pp. 139–41.
6 Ibid., p. 141.
7 Civil Service Commission, *The Civil Service* (Fullon Report), vol. 1 (HMSO, 1968). Appendix B, p. 108; my italics.
8 H. C. G. Matthew, *Gladstone 1809–1874* (Oxford University Press paperback, Oxford, 1988), p. 85.
9 Ibid., p. 116.
10 Frank Prokashka, 'Philanthropy', in F. M. L. Thompson (ed.), *The Cambridge Social History of Britain 1750–1950*, vol. 3: *Social Agencies and Institutions* (Cambridge University Press, Cambridge, 1990), pp. 357–93.
11 Asa Briggs, *Victorian Cities* (Odhams Press, London, 1963), p. 221.
12 Ibid., pp. 208–9.
13 Harold Perkin, *The Rise of Professional Society: England since 1880* (Routledge, London and New York, 1989).
14 Quoted in ibid., p. 128.
15 Marshall, *Citizenship and Social Class*, p. 136.

Chapter 3   Troubled Zenith

1   Quoted in Perkin, *Rise of Professional Society*, p. 406.
2   Anthony Crosland, *The Future of Socialism*, repr. in Riesman (ed.), *Theories of the Mixed Economy* (William Pickering, London, 1994), p. 37.
3   Perkin, *Rise of Professional Society*, pp. 405–6.
4   Gabriel Almond and Sidney Verba, *The Civic Culture: Political Attitudes and Democracy in Five Nations* (Princeton University Press, Princeton, NJ, 1963), pp. 108 and 185.
5   Samuel H. Beer and Adam B. Ulam, *Patterns of Government: The Major Political Systems of Europe* (Random House, New York, 1962), p. 76.
6   L. S. Amery, *Thoughts on the Constitution* (Oxford University Press, Oxford, 1947), pp. 14–18.
7   For a fuller discussion of these data and their implications see my *The Unprincipled Society: New Demands and Old Politics* (Jonathan Cape, London, 1988), pp. 191–6.
8   Richard Sennett, *The Fall of Public Man*, paperback edition (Faber & Faber, London, 1993).
9   Anthony Barnett, *This Time: Our Constitutional Revolution* (Vintage, London, 1997), pp. 116–17.
10   Peter Jenkins, *The Battle of Downing Street* (Charles Knight, London, 1970), ch. 5.
11   Sennett, *Fall of Public Man*, p. 25.
12   Ibid., p. 265.

Chapter 4   *Kulturkampf*

1   Margaret Thatcher, *The Path to Power* (HarperCollins, London, 1995), p. 565.
2   Quoted in Ian Gilmour, *Dancing with Dogma* (Simon & Schuster, London, 1992), p. 105.
3   Shirley Letwin, *The Anatomy of Thatcherism* (Fontana Press, London, 1992), p. 33.
4   F. A. Hayek, *Law, Legislation and Liberty*, vol. 3: *The Political Order of a Free People* (Routledge & Kegan Paul, London, 1979), pp. 112–27.

5 Kenneth Minogue, 'The Emergence of the New Right', in Robert Skidelsky (ed.), *Thatcherism* (Chatto and Windus, London, 1988), pp. 141–2.

6 Simon Jenkins, *Accountable to None: The Tory Nationalisation of Britain* (Hamish Hamilton, London, 1995), p. 8.

7 Quoted in Peter Wiles, 'A Syndrome, Not a Doctrine: Some Elementary Theses on Populism', in Ghita Ionescu and Ernest Gellner (eds), *Populism: Its National Characteristics* (Weidenfeld and Nicolson, London, 1969), p. 166.

8 Egon Wertheimer, *Portrait of the Labour Party* (G. P. Putnam's Sons, London, 1929), p. 177.

9 Lord Young of Graffham, 'Enterprise Regained', in Paul Heelas and Paul Morris (eds), *The Values of the Enterprise Culture: The Moral Debate* (Routledge, London and New York, 1992), p. 29.

10 Nigel Lawson, *The View From No. 11*, paperback edition (Corgi Books, London, 1993), pp. 64–5; my italics.

11 Simon Jenkins, *Accountable to None*; John Kay, www. privatisation.uk.com.

12 Quoted in Hugo Young, *One of Us* (Macmillan, London, 1989), p. 232.

13 Michael Power, *The Audit Explosion* (Demos, London, 1994).

14 Ibid., pp. 48–9.

15 Charles Webster, *The National Health Service: A Political History*, 2nd edition (Oxford University Press, Oxford, 2002), p. 141.

16 Simon Jenkins, *Accountable to None*, p. 83.

17 Webster, *National Health Service*, p. 198.

18 Quoted in Simon Jenkins, *Accountable to None*, p. 106, my italics.

Chapter 5   Counter-Attack

1 Catherine Needham, *Citzen-consumers: New Labour's Marketplace Democracy* (The Catalyst Forum, London, 2003), pp. 17–23.

2 Philip Gould, *The Unfinished Revolution: How the Modernisers Saved the Labour Party* (Little, Brown and Co., London, 1998), especially pp. 391–9.

3   Alexis de Tocqueville, *Democracy in America*, ed. Alan Ryan (Everyman's Library, London, 1994), pp. 318–19.
4   Tony Travers 'Local Government', in *The Blair Effect: the Blair Government 1997–2001*, ed. Anthony Seldon, (Little, Brown and Co., London, 2001), p. 133.
5   Speech of 7 February 2003.www.hm-treasury.gov.uk/ newsroom_and_speeches/press/2003.
6   www.publications.parliament.uk/pa/cm200203/cmhansard/ cm030507/debtext/30507.
7   Rod Rhodes, 'The Civil Service', in *Blair Effect*, ed. Seldon, p. 102.
8   http://www.mori.com/polls/trends/trust.shtml.
9   Henley Centre Dataculture, 1996.
10 *British Social Attitudes* (Gower, Aldershot, 1987 and 1997).
11 *State of the Nation*, ICM for the Joseph Rowntree Reform Trust, 2000.
12 Peter A. Hall, 'Social Capital in Britain', *British Journal of Political Science*, 29 (1900), pp. 417–61.
13 See Michael Power, *The Audit Society: Rituals of Verification* (Oxford University Press, Oxford, 1997).
14 Albert Weale, *The New Politics of Pollution* (Manchester University Press, Manchester and New York, 1992), p. 221.
15 For an excellent discussion of new forms of accountability see Power, *Audit Explosion*.
16 Quoted in Robert Watt, 'The Crown and its Employees', in Maurice Sunkin and Sebastian Payne, *The Nature of the Crown: A Legal and Political Analysis* (Oxford University Press, Oxford, 1999), p. 288. In the passages that follow I draw heavily on this book.
17 Rodney Brazier, 'Constitutional Reform and the Crown', in Sunkin and Payne, *Nature of the Crown*, pp. 350–4.

Select Bibliography

Almond, Gabriel and Sidney Verba, *The Civic Culture: Political Attitudes and Democracy in Five Nations*, Princeton University Press, Princeton, NJ, 1963.

Amery, L. S., *Thoughts on the Constitution*, Oxford University Press, Oxford, 1947.

Bagehot, Walter, *The English Constitution*, ed. R. H. S. Crossman, Fontana/Collins, Glasgow, 1963.

Barnett, Anthony, *This Time: Our Constitutional Revolution*, Vintage, London, 1997.

Beer, Samuel H. and Adam B. Ulam, *Patterns of Government: The Major Political Systems of Europe*, Random House, New York, 1962.

Beetham, David et al., *Democracy under Blair: A Democratic Audit of the United Kingdom*, Politicos, London, 2002.

Bobbit, Philip, *The Shield of Achilles: War, Peace and the Course of History*, Penguin Books, London, 2003.

Bridges, Baron Edward, *Portrait of a Profession: The Civil Service Tradition*, Cambridge University Press, Cambridge, 1950.

Briggs, Asa, *Victorian Cities*, Odhams Press, London, 1963.

British Social Attitudes, Gower, Aldershot, 1987 and 1997.

Brittan, Samuel, *The Economic Consequences of Democracy*, Temple Smith, London, 1977.

Broadbent, Jane, Michael Dietrich and Jennifer Roberts (eds), *The End of the Professions?: The Restructuring of Professional Work*, Routledge, London and New York, 1997.

Select Bibliography

Building Better Partnerships: The Final Report of the Commission on Public Private Partnerships, IPPR, London, n.d.

Cairncross, Alec, *Years of Recovery: British Economic Policy, 1945–51*, Methuen, London, 1985.

Chapman, Richard A., *Ethics in the British Civil Service*, Routledge, London, 1988.

Chester, Sir Norman, *The English Administrative System, 1780–1870*, Clarendon Press, Oxford, 1981.

Cockett, Richard, *Thinking the Unthinkable: Think Tanks and the Economic Counter-Revolution*, HarperCollins, London, 1995.

Crosland, Anthony, *The Future of Socialism*, reprinted in David Riesman (ed.), *Theories of the Mixed Economy*, William Pickering, London, 1994.

Dahrendorf, Ralph et al., *Report on Wealth Creation and Social Cohesion in a Free Society*, privately printed, London, 1995.

D'Arcy, Mark and Rory Maclean, *Nightmare: The Race to Become London's Mayor*, Politicos, London, 2000.

De Tocqueville, Alexis, *Democracy in America*, ed. Alan Ryan, Everyman's Library, London, 1994.

Gamble, Andrew, *The Free Economy and the Strong State: The Politics of Thatcherism*, 2nd edition, Macmillan, Basingstoke, 1994.

Gilmour, Ian, *Dancing with Dogma*, Simon & Schuster, London, 1992.

Gould, Philip, *The Unfinished Revolution: How the Modernisers Saved the Labour Party*, Little, Brown and Co., London, 1998.

Greenleaf, W. H., *The British Political Tradition*, vol. 1: *The Rise of Collectivism*, Methuen, London, 1983.

Hall, Peter A., 'Social Capital in Britain', *British Journal of Political Science*, 29 (1900), 417–61.

Harris, José, *Private Lives, Public Spirit: A Social History of Britain 1870–1914*, Penguin Books, Harmondsworth, 1994.

Hayek, F. A., *Law, Legislation and Liberty*, vol. 3: *The Political Order of a Free People*, Routledge & Kegan Paul, London, 1979.

Heelas, Paul and Paul Morris (eds), *The Values of the Enterprise Culture: The Moral Debate*, Routledge, London and New York, 1992.

Hennessy, Peter, *Whitehall*, paperback edition, Fontana Press, London, 1990.

Hobhouse, L. T., *Liberalism*, Oxford University Press, London, 1911.

Hood, Christopher, *The Art of the State: Culture, Rhetoric and Public Management*, Clarendon Press, Oxford, 2000.

Ionescu, Ghita and Ernest Gellner (eds), *Populism: Its National Characteristics*, Weidenfeld and Nicolson, London, 1969.

Jenkins, Peter, *The Battle of Downing Street*, Charles Knight, London, 1970.

Jenkins, Simon, *Accountable to None: The Tory Nationalisation of Britain*, Hamish Hamilton, London, 1995.

Kay, John, *The Truth about Markets: Their Genius, their Limits, their Follies*, Allen Lane, London, 2003.

Klein, Rudolf, *The Politics of the National Health Service*, Longman, London, 1983.

Lawson, Nigel, *The View from No. 11*, paperback edition, Corgi Books, London, 1993.

Letwin, Shirley, *The Anatomy of Thatcherism*, Fontana Press, London, 1992.

Leys, Colin, *Market-Driven Politics, Neoliberal Democracy and the Public Interest*, Verso, London and New York, 2001.

The London Underground Public Private Partnership: An Independent Review, The Industrial Society, London, 2000.

Marquand, David, *The Unprincipled Society: New Demands and Old Politics*, Jonathan Cape, London, 1988.

Marquand, David, *Populism or Pluralism? New Labour and the Constitution*, The Constitution Unit, School of Public Policy, University College London, London, 1999.

Marshall, T. H., *Citizenship and Social Class and Other Essays*, Cambridge University Press, Cambridge, 1950.

Matthew, H. C. G., *Gladstone 1809–1874*, Oxford University Press paperback, Oxford, 1988.

Matthew, H. C. G., *Gladstone 1875–1898*, Clarendon Press, Oxford, 1995.

Maxwell, Robert J., *An Unplayable Hand? BSE, CJD and the British Government*, King's Fund, London, 1997.

Moggridge, D. E., *Maynard Keynes: An Economist's Biography*, Routledge, London and New York, 1992.

Mount, Ferdinand, *The British Constitution Now*, Heinemann, London, 1992.

Namier, L. B., *England in the Age of the American Revolution*, Macmillan, London, 1930.

Namier, Sir Lewis, *The Structure of Politics at the Accession of George III*, 2nd edition, Macmillan, London, 1957.

Needham, Catherine, *Citizen-consumers: New Labour's Marketplace Democracy*, The Catalyst Forum, London, 2003.

Norton-Taylor, Richard, Mark Lloyd and Stephen Cook, *Knee Deep in Dishonour: The Scott Report and its Aftermath*, Victor Gollancz, London, 1996.

Nye, Joseph S., Philip D. Zeliko and David C. King (eds), *Why People Don't Trust Government*, Harvard University Press, Cambridge, Mass., 1997.

Oldfield, Adrian, *Citizenship and Community: Civic Republicanism and the Modern World*, Routledge, London and New York, 1990.

O'Neill, Onora, *A Question of Trust*, BBC Reith Lectures 2002, Cambridge University Press, Cambridge, 2002.

Perkin, Harold, *The Origins of Modern English Society 1780–1880*, paperback edition, Routledge & Kegan Paul, London, 1972.

Perkin, Harold, *The Rise of Professional Society: England since 1880*, Routledge, London and New York, 1989.

Pettit, Philip, *Republicanism: A Theory of Freedom and Government*, Oxford University Press, Oxford, 1997.

Pimlott, Ben and Nirmala Rao, *Governing London*, Oxford University Press, Oxford, 2002.

Pocock, J. G. A., *The Machiavellian Moment: Florentine Political Thought and the Atlantic Republican Tradition*, Princeton University Press, Princeton, NJ, 1975.

Polanyi, Karl, *The Great Transformation: The Political and Economic Origins of our Time*, Beacon paperback edition, Boston, 1957.

Power, Michael, *The Audit Explosion*, Demos, London, 1994.

Power, Michael, *The Audit Society: Rituals of Verification*, Oxford University Press, Oxford, 1997.

Prokashka, Frank, 'Philanthropy', in F. M. L. Thompson (ed.), *The Cambridge Social History of Britain 1750–1950*, vol. 3: *Social Agencies and Institutions*, Cambridge University Press, Cambridge, 1990.

Public Law, special issue on the Scott Report, 1996.

Putnam, Robert D., *Bowling Alone: The Collapse and Revival of American Community*, Simon & Schuster, New York, 2000.

Select Bibliography

Report of the Inquiry into the Export of Defence Equipment and Dual-Use Goods to Iraq and Related Prosecutions, by the Rt. Hon. Sir Richard Scott, the Vice-Chancellor (the Scott Report), HMSO, London, 1996.

Report, Evidence and Supporting Papers of the Inquiry into the Emergence and Identification of Bovine Spongiform Encephalopathy (BSE) and Variant Creutzfeldt–Jakob Disease (vCJD) and the Action Taken in Response to it up to 20 March 1966 (the Phillips Report), HMSO, London, October 2000, vol. 1.

Rhodes, R. A. W., 'The Hollowing Out of the State', *Political Quarterly*, 65 (1900), 138–51.

Richards, David, *The Civil Service under the Conservatives 1979–1997*, Sussex Academic Press, Brighton, 1997.

Ridley, Rosalind M., and Harry F. Baker, *Fatal Protein: The Story of CJD, BSE and Other Prion Diseases*, Oxford University Press, Oxford, 1998.

Schumpeter, Joseph, *Capitalism, Socialism and Democracy*, George Allen and Unwin, London, 1979.

Seldon, Anthony (ed.), *The Blair Effect: The Blair Government 1997–2001*, Little, Brown and Co., London, 2001.

Sennett, Richard, *The Fall of Public Man*, paperback edition, Faber & Faber, London, 1993.

Skidelsky, Robert (ed.), *Thatcherism*, Chatto and Windus, London, 1988.

Skinner, Quentin, *Liberty before Liberalism*, Cambridge University Press, Cambridge, 1998.

Smith, Martin J., *The Core Executive in Britain*, Macmillan, Basingstoke, 1999.

State of the Nation, ICM for the Joseph Rowntree Reform Trust, 2000.

Sunkin, Maurice and Sebastian Payne, *The Nature of the Crown: A Legal and Political Analysis*, Oxford University Press, Oxford, 1999.

Tawney, R. H., *The Acquisitive Society*, Bell, London, 1921.

Tawney, R. H., *Equality*, reprinted in David Riesman (ed.), *Theories of the Mixed Economy*, William Pickering, London, 1994.

Thatcher, Margaret, *The Path to Power*, HarperCollins, London, 1995.

Select Bibliography

Thompson, Brian and F. F. Ridley, *Under the Scott-Light: British Government Seen through the Scott Report*, Oxford University Press, Oxford, 1997.

Thompson, E. P., *Whigs and Hunters: The Origins of the Black Acts*, Allen Lane, London, 1975.

Timmins, Nicholas, *The Five Giants: A Biography of the Welfare State*, Fontana Press, London, 1996.

Titmuss, Richard, *Commitment to Welfare*, reprinted in David Riesman (ed.), *Theories of the Mixed Economy*, William Pickering, London, 1994.

Trilling, Lionel, *Sincerity and Authenticity*, Oxford University Press, London, 1974.

Walzer, Michael, *Spheres of Justice: A Defence of Pluralism and Equality*, Basic Books, New York, 1983.

Weale, Albert, *The New Politics of Pollution*, Manchester University Press, Manchester and New York, 1992.

Webster, Charles, *The National Health Service: A Political History*, 2nd edition, Oxford University Press, Oxford, 2002.

Wertheimer, Egon, *Portrait of the Labour Party*, G. P. Putnam's Sons, London, 1929.

Wolmar, Christian, *Down the Tube: The Battle for London's Underground*, Aurum Press, London, 2002.

Young, Hugo, *One of Us*, Macmillan, London, 1989.

Index

Index

163

Index

Index